Unless -R̶

THE BIG TEN

ALSO BY JEFFREY E. GARTEN

A Cold Peace:
America, Japan, Germany, and the Struggle for Supremacy

Jeffrey E. Garten

The BIG

TEN

THE BIG

EMERGING

MARKETS

AND HOW THEY WILL

CHANGE OUR LIVES

📚 BasicBooks
A Division of HarperCollins*Publishers*

Copyright © 1997 by Jeffrey E. Garten.

Published by BasicBooks,
A Division of HarperCollins Publishers, Inc.

FIRST EDITION

Designed by Elliott Beard

Library of Congress Cataloging-in-Publication Data
Garten, Jeffrey E.
    The big ten: the big emerging markets and how they will change
our lives / by Jeffrey E. Garten.
        p.   cm.
    Includes bibliographical references and index.
    ISBN 0-465-02651-6
    1. United States—Commerce—Developing countries—Fore-
casting. 2. Developing countries—Commerce—United States—Forecasting. 3. United States—Foreign economic relations—Developing
countries—Forecasting. 4. Developing countries—Foreign economic
relations—United States—Forecasting.   I. Title.
HF4055.037 1997
382'.0973—dc21   97-2011

97 98 99 00 01 ❖/RRD 10 9 8 7 6 5 4 3 2 1

For Ina

Contents

Acknowledgments

I AM DEEPLY INDEBTED to my former colleagues at the U.S. Department of Commerce who helped conceive and implement the "Big Emerging Markets" strategy. Without the dynamic political leadership of Secretary of Commerce Ronald H. Brown, and the extraordinary energy and creativity of my deputy, David Rothkopf, we could never have launched or sustained the "BEMs" project. As head of our Public Affairs office, Cécile Ablack did a tremendous job in presenting our message from Baltimore to Bombay. Highly skilled political appointees Lauri Fitz-Pagado, Robert LaRussa, Raymond Vickery, and Clyde Robinson, as well as dedicated civil servants Timothy Hauser, Donald Forrest, Jonathan Menes, Karen Goddin, Richard Harding, Anne Hughes, Walter Sabastain, Regina Vargo, and Frank Vargo were among the key officials who made the strategy work. In fact, the entire 2,500-member International Trade Administration, which I led in the Commerce Department, with people stationed throughout the United States and the world, was heavily involved and supportive, and they provided an extraordinary public service for the country.

I would also like to thank several very talented students for their research assistance on this book. They are Brad Ellis, S. Keiler Snow, and Stewart Stewart from the Yale School of Management. I am especially indebted to Amy Auster from Columbia's School of International and Public Affairs, who did significant research on individual countries, and who prepared the appendix. And I am very grateful to Mary Ann Green, my assistant, who worked long nights for many months to produce successive drafts of this book.

Paul Golob of Basic Books has been a superb editor—tough, thoughtful, responsive. He encouraged me to write this book, and helped me with every draft of it, and I wish to express my thanks to him for all his assistance.

Finally, I have had a terrific agent, Raphael Sagalyn, whose advice went well beyond book contracts, and I am most grateful to him.

New Haven, Connecticut
February 1997

Introduction: America's Challenge

MANY OF US HAVE had the experience of sitting on the beach on a bright, warm day when dark clouds suddenly move in, the sun disappears, and rain pours down. The change in weather can happen very fast, catching us totally unprepared as everyone scrambles for cover and frantically gathers up clothes, books, radios, umbrellas. At the shore, the experience of such abrupt change doesn't carry with it great consequences. But a country can be caught by surprise, too, and then, of course, the stakes are much higher. That is what could easily happen to the United States. In place of clouds, there are new, powerful global forces gathering. They are embodied by the rise of ten big emerging markets—countries like China, India, and Brazil—which are acquiring enough power to change the face of global politics and economies. These up-and-coming countries could provide great opportunities for America—expanding markets for our products, higher returns on our investments, and new friends in building a more peaceful and prosperous world. But they could also pose great risks—political and economic turmoil, challenges to our quest for free markets and democracy, assaults on our standards of human rights, and threats to our national security. Dealing with the big emerging markets will be the key to our economic well-being and to our security in the decades ahead. It will require a new mind-set about our economic and social policies as well as fresh strategies for our involvement overseas. America is totally unprepared for this challenge.

But before I tell the story, let me explain how and why I came to write it.

When I entered the Clinton administration as Under Secretary of Commerce for International Trade in the summer of 1993, I brought with me the experience of having served in the Nixon, Ford, and Carter governments and also having worked on Wall Street for thirteen years as an investment banker with a focus on global finance. I came to Washington believing that America's position in the world was changing fast. Fundamental interests were shifting not only from the previous preoccupation with the former Soviet Union, but also away from Western Europe and Japan to other regions of the world, such as Asia, Latin America, and Central Europe, where economic growth would be much stronger, where markets were more vibrant, and where new political power was accumulating. Such shifts had profound implications for every aspect of America's role in the world: We would have to reorient our foreign policy priorities and we would have to think differently about trade, finance, political involvement, and military security, as well as the whole range of economic and social policies at home that might affect our competitiveness and our economic security. The task facing the new administration was to convince the Congress to pay more attention to these challenges, and to make our case to the American public, which was distracted by so many other issues.

In my first set of meetings with my new boss, Secretary of Commerce Ronald H. Brown, he and I discussed the idea of this massive shift in American global interests. Brown's instincts were the same as mine, and he urged me to undertake an intensive analysis in order to see whether we could prove our case. Look over the horizon, he suggested, and ask the fundamental questions, "Where will American interests in the world lie ten or twenty years from now? What should be our longer-term goals, and how can we achieve them?" For the following five months this project became my obsession. I was able to gather excellent people from around the administration to think through where the country should be headed in the international arena. We had access to an enormous amount of information—the experienced analysts in the departments of Commerce, State, Treasury, and the C.I.A.; exceptionally bright young government professionals whom we discovered buried in the bureaucracy; the resources of our embassies around the world; research done in America's best think tanks; views of top executives in dynamic companies doing business abroad. We looked at overall trends. We examined specific countries.

It was an effort that was exhilarating and exhausting—one of the most intense periods of my life. I would awaken regularly at 4 A.M. in order to review and comment on the papers that had been prepared the day before so that there would be no delay in proceeding when the office reopened at 8:30. Often we had far too much information, and a key challenge became figuring out what constituted a real trend as opposed to an interesting but one-time event. We looked at the industrialized world, the former communist nations, the developing countries.

By the end of the five months we concluded that a new world was indeed arising. In the future there would be a new category of country with which America would have to contend. Some ten nations were at the heart of this group, and we called them the "big emerging markets."

All of these "BEMs" were big, ambitious, and gaining power in their geographical neighborhoods. They were looking for their place in the sun, and forcing others to make room. They were increasingly aggressive and influential. There were some obvious candidates such as China, India, Indonesia, and Brazil, all with huge populations and land mass, impressive economic progress, and enormous political ambition. But the "Big Ten" also included Mexico and Argentina in our hemisphere, South Africa in Africa, Poland and Turkey in Europe, and South Korea in Asia.

Selecting who qualified as a BEM and who did not was agonizing. Some of my colleagues argued for the inclusion of Russia. Others asked why we would include India and not Pakistan. These were tough questions and forced us to think hard about defining our criteria for selection. But in the end we believed that we had picked ten big emerging markets that would be critical to the evolution of the world for the rest of the 1990s and several decades beyond, and that would also be at the center of many of America's most vital concerns at home and abroad. For example, we selected countries that would determine in large part what the global trade and financial system would look like, and countries that simultaneously would hold the key to war and peace in crucial hotspots around the world. Our list contained BEMs that would be central to global efforts to improve human rights, safeguard the environment, and deal with narcotics trafficking.

When our study was completed, Secretary Brown presented the results at a cabinet meeting. He received unanimous encouragement to develop a comprehensive BEM strategy. Because of his mandate at the Commerce Department to handle commercial policies, Brown focused his presentation mostly on America's opportunities to expand its exports to the BEMs. Nevertheless, he and I knew that the implications of a Big Emerging Market strategy would be much broader than merely selling U.S. products, for exports were the tip of the iceberg in the kinds of engagement we would need with the BEMs. We knew it would be necessary for Washington to help American firms break into the markets in the first place, raising all kinds of ideological and practical issues about what kind of help government should give to business in our society. We would have to facilitate closer ties between the business sectors of America and local firms in the BEMs, since the private sector was where the action would be abroad, now that private capital was so much more important than financing from governments, and that state-owned companies were being sold off to private investors. We would need to think about technical assistance to help countries develop mechanisms to protect patents, copyrights, and trademarks, and to build modern stock markets. We would have to find ways to help countries make the transition from government-dominated to free market economies, recognizing the enormous sensitivities of involving ourselves in the internal affairs of other countries.

Moreover, we believed that broad economic ties would become the pivot around which all other aspects of our relations with these countries would revolve—political and military links, as well as cooperation and conflict over human rights, fair treatment for workers, sharing technology, environmental protection, drug trafficking, terrorism. We anticipated that some of America's most intractable dilemmas in the years ahead would arise because of the difficulty of pursuing so many goals in the BEMs at one time.

Indeed, we knew that any substantial engagement with the big emerging markets would raise questions that could be resolved only through trial and error, success and failure. How much trade pressure could we put on countries like Brazil or South Africa without straining the overall relationships that were becoming so important to us? How much technology could we sell to China or South Korea without undermining our own competitiveness? Would it be possible to balance concerns over human rights with the need to win foreign markets or cooperate on military matters?

And as our policies evolved, a second set of issues arose concerning the proper relations between government and business. In helping American firms to penetrate foreign markets, what ought to be the guidelines to insure that the United States as a whole benefited, and not just an individual company? And how were we to address the allegation that any help that Washington provides to American companies is "corporate welfare"?

Though the headlines were dominated by the war in Bosnia or trade disputes with Japan, Secretary Brown and I believed that the ups and downs of our engagement with the BEMs—with the combination of economic, social, political, and security dimensions—would become the *fundamental* international issue for America in the next two decades. And so, during my tenure in the first Clinton administration, with Brown's strong support I spent nearly all of my time focusing on the evolution of a comprehensive American strategy toward the BEMs.

I participated in interagency debates, held under the auspices of the National Security Council or the National Economic Council, concerning trade policy toward several big emerging markets. From the Commerce Department I oversaw intergovernmental task forces to reexamine our commercial strategy toward every one of the Big Ten. Each task force conducted an exhaustive study that tried to look a decade into the future and come to grips with economic and political trends, as well as make the best quantification we could of the opportunities for American firms.

My colleagues and I also reorganized the U.S. Commercial Service—the 1,000 men and women stationed around the U.S. and the world whose job it is to promote U.S. exports—to give primary emphasis to helping American companies to sell their products to all ten big emerging markets. For most BEMs, we established a joint council between their government and the U.S. government—such as the Business Development Committee with Brazil, or the U.S.–Indian Commercial Alliance—all designed to bring governments and private sectors together to increase trade and investment, and to build stronger economic ties.

Among our most significant accomplishments was the establishment of a special center within the Department of Commerce to help American firms win big commercial contracts in an environment of brutal competition among U.S., European, and Japanese companies. Officially called the "Advocacy Center," this new operation looked and functioned more like a Wall Street trading floor than a government office, and it came to be called the "economic war room." It brought together all parts of the administration—the departments of State, Treasury, and Commerce, the Export-Import Bank, other government financing agencies, and our ambassadors around the world. It became the nerve center for the BEM strategy and a place with which American companies could easily connect as a central coordinating point. Everyone in the public and private sector involved with the war room had a single objective—to win deals for American companies bidding against other nations' firms that were supported by *their* governments.

My colleagues and I did a lot of traveling. We blanketed the U.S., consulting with American firms, exchanging views with thousands of Americans at chambers of commerce and other business gatherings, as well as councils on foreign relations. We spent a good deal of time in Latin America and Asia, including working with Secretary Brown on major trade missions that included top American CEOs to China, India, and Brazil. In these and other overseas visits—many of them extending for two weeks at a time—I was able to confer with presidents, prime ministers, central bankers, and large numbers of top American and foreign business leaders. Every trip, whether to Chicago or Shanghai, contributed to my understanding of America's changing role in the world, and the crucial importance of the BEMs in how we should think about the future.

The first Clinton administration made an excellent start in reorienting American foreign policy to take account of the big emerging markets, devising a comprehensive export strategy for each BEM and beginning the difficult task of reorienting the entire government bureaucracy to execute strategic plans for the Big Ten. But for several reasons, it was just a start.

In the first place, the BEM strategy was defined too narrowly. Exports are crucial to the U.S. economy, to be sure, but the Big Ten compel a much more expansive definition of U.S. interests. It is true that exports have been a powerful source of American economic growth and a generator of good jobs at home. And it is certainly the case that the United States is locked into fierce competition with Europe and Japan for foreign markets. But America must be much more than the world's number one salesman. Japan or France may define their interests in predominantly commercial terms. But the country that led the efforts to smash German Nazism, Japanese militarism, and Russian communism in the last half-century alone, and that today stands as the only true super-power, and as a beacon for freedom around the world, must take a broader view of its role.

Second, most of the foreign-policy establishment still accords disproportionate emphasis to maintaining smooth relations with our traditional allies. These foreign policy "pros" are content to watch Washington promote exports to emerging markets, but they still consider commercial activity a sideshow to the really important business of military treaties or political summits. For these traditionalists, it would be far too radical to accord the full range of political and economic considerations to the big emerging markets that are routinely applied to a country like England or Germany. The emerging markets are not seen as being *that* important. They are too distant, too different from us, too unstable. Moreover, the big policy issues are more complicated than the diplomacy that most of our State Department has known these past several decades, for they involve intricate trade and investment issues, intellectual property rights, labor standards, human rights, technology transfer, corruption, and environmental protection all colliding with each other at the same time, and requiring agonizing trade-offs. This would rarely happen with our close allies.

Another area that needed more attention from the administration was the linkage between our international commercial diplomacy, which was aimed at expanding trade, and the economic and social policies at home needed to help Americans deal with the dislocations caused by increasing imports. In most of the high-level policy discussions in which I participated, the two dimensions of policy were not adequately joined, for top officials from the departments of Labor, Health and Human Services, and Education, all with something to say about enhancing America's economic security, were rarely present. But when I spoke to Americans in Boston or San Diego, issues like NAFTA and growing imports from Mexico, or the rising trade deficits with China, always revealed deep domestic anxieties about the future.

Moreover, when certain aspects of the Big Emerging Markets strategy came under attack, the administration did not mount a coordinated defense, let alone an aggressive one. The first salvo was the effort by the new Republican Congress in 1995 to dismantle the Commerce Department, on the grounds that its functions, including trade promotion, were merely subsidies to American business. While it was true that the department could have been significantly streamlined and made even more effective, the notion that America should unilaterally disarm itself in the brutally competitive global commercial arena at the moment when the Europeans and Japanese were expanding their government-sponsored activities was absurd. Secretary Brown defended our efforts tirelessly, but other cabinet officials did not provide strong support and the President missed an opportunity to articulate the importance of an even more aggressive international commercial effort. The department survived, as did the big emerging markets strategy, but both were greatly weakened.

Finally, in the presidential campaign of 1996, the BEMs strategy became a political hot potato, as news reports about illegal campaign contributions from Asian sources (especially Indonesia) led to mounting concerns that the Clinton administration's trade and foreign policy might have been improperly influenced. No one could deny that campaign laws needed to be tightened, or that government officials ought to take more precautions to ensure that every aspect of our policies toward the big emerging markets was conducted according to the highest standards of integrity. But the scandals of 1996 do not change the fact that the BEMs remain vital to America's national interest, nor that we must continue to seek ways to more closely engage these nations.

I have written this book to try to carry the discussion of America's role in the world further than I believe it has gone in the public arena. I make no pretense of having produced an exhaustive study, and certainly not a scholarly one. Every chapter—indeed, even sections of chapters—could be a book in itself. I am aware of the risks of generalization when discussing ten countries, each with different histories, different political and economic systems, different cultures. But at a time when we are all so bombarded with specialized information from newspapers, magazines, faxes, television, and the Internet, it has become more difficult to discern the big picture, and there remains a need to try to present a framework for a very large set of issues in a book that can be read in one or two sittings. In this regard I take heart from advice that Jack Welch, Chairman of General Electric, and one of America's great CEOs, gave to his staff: "Have the courage to keep it simple." I'm also conscious that Albert Einstein was also alleged to have said, "Make it as simple as possible, but no more so." I've tried to walk this tightrope with full knowledge that it's impossible not to occasionally fall off.

Although it came as no surprise that the recent presidential election highlighted the emptiness of what passes for political leadership these days, the bigger problem is that neither of our two major political parties has an outlook or a strategy that takes into account both our domestic needs and the rapidly changing international context in which they will have to be met. At the end of the last congress, and during the presidential campaign, we were treated to a massive wave of social legislation as well as tax and spending proposals. Who could tell what they meant, let alone their connection to the broader international setting? Who knew whether they were proportional to our problems or merely sound bites to fill the evening news? Who could get the sense that there was a strong link between the great political and economic openings in South Africa, Argentina, and India, and our future at home? Or between the political and economic tensions in South Korea and Indonesia, and the stability of world trade and politics?

We seem inured to the shortcomings and the shenanigans of our national political leadership, but being accustomed to this behavior does not mean that all is well, or even that the status quo will be maintained. In fact, I believe that there is a dangerous complacency in the United States today. Yes, we are the world's most powerful nation. Our firms are supercompetitive. The countries that many of us worried about as potential rivals, such as Japan or Germany, seem to be mired in a host of problems. And the American economy is reasonably strong, growing steadily with low inflation and low unemployment. So why even bother to focus more attention on the changing global arena?

There is only one answer: The current environment is much more fragile than it appears. The pace of the American economy exceeds that of Europe or Japan, but the fact remains that we are expanding at the slowest rate in many decades, and much of our growth is tied to exports, which themselves depend on continued economic progress in big emerging markets. American business has been in a modest expansionary stage for a long time now, because some unique factors have been at play. The federal budget deficit has been reduced in huge increments, but that dramatic pattern cannot be maintained. Corporate downsizing has made a dramatic contribution to American competitiveness, but it has reached a dangerous level. A booming stock market has boosted corporate fortunes and individual wealth, but our history is replete with large "market corrections." A hike in U.S. interest rates combined with a drop in exports could change our domestic picture very quickly and dramatically for the worse. And unless the pattern of business cycles has ended forever—a sharp departure from hundreds of years of economic history—a recession cannot be ruled out, sooner rather than later. Were the economy to go into reverse gear, today's layoffs and economic anxieties would soar, optimism about the United States would plummet, and our entire view of the global environment would quickly turn sour.

We should also remember that international conditions change very rapidly, and it has proved impossible for anyone to forecast important developments with any accuracy. Hardly anyone thought that a desperate group of underdeveloped oil-producing countries could band together and hold up America, Europe, and Japan as OPEC did in the 1970s. Try identifying someone who predicted the powerful emergence of Japan in the 1980s, or the stunning rise of the Asian tigers—South Korea, Taiwan, Hong Kong, and Singapore. Few experts foresaw the quick and decisive liberation of all of Eastern Europe and the implosion of the former Soviet Union. The onset of global inflation in the 1970s, the drop in productivity in the industrial nations in the 1990s, the coming of the Internet and all its ramifications—all these were a surprise even to the most knowledgeable observers. Thinking about the present, it is almost impossible to recall a period in this century when there were so many changes in the world occurring at one time—new countries, new leaders, new philosophies, new technologies. It is surely dangerous to bank on the fact that the United States will occupy so favorable a position a decade from now, at least not without a more deliberate strategy than it now has.

And then there is the question of how favorable our position really is. For all the current optimism, none of the big budget issues have been tackled yet—not social security, not health care, not America's soaring needs for repair and modernization of schools, highways, bridges, and airports. In the late 1980s there was a vigorous debate about the need to deal with education, crime, drugs, and child poverty. It's not that these issues are being ignored by the political leadership, for the front pages are full of public concerns. The fact is, however, that the problems remain, and they are still very severe by any standards. A coherent set of philosophies or programs to address our social agenda is nowhere in sight. Given that the essence of America's global strength is its strength at home, we ought to remain concerned about the depth of our shortcomings. And every one of these problems is going to undercut our ability to deal with the rise of the BEMs, representing as it does the challenge of maintaining our power and our prosperity in a rapidly changing global economy from which our lives and our futures can no longer be separated.

We are in the midst of cataclysmic change that will result in a new map of power and influence, a map being redrawn by the big emerging markets. It is a revolution as significant in its implications as the great historical shifts such as the breakdown of feudalism, the two past industrial revolutions, the growth of a global economy in the nineteenth century, and the collapse of the old order in the 1930s and 1940s. The crucial question is: Will America be up to the challenge?

THE BIG TEN

1 | Who Are the Big Emerging Markets, and Why Are They Important?

Ten big emerging markets, located in every part of the world, will change the face of global economics and politics. They are: Mexico, Brazil, Argentina, South Africa, Poland, Turkey, India, Indonesia, China, and South Korea.

Each big emerging market is important as an individual country; but it is the combined effect of the group as a whole that will have a critical impact on American interests at home and abroad.

The big emerging markets are the key swing factor in the future growth of world trade, global financial stability, and the transition to free market economies in Asia, Central Europe, and Latin America. They are also crucial to nuclear nonproliferation, the improvement of human rights, environmental cooperation, and the avoidance of war in several critical hotspots.

THE BIG EMERGING MARKETS (BEMs) are often in the news these days, but without a broader framework for thinking about them, the stories appear far less significant than they are. When the Mexican economy went into a tailspin in 1995, it looked like a story about Mexico, but in fact that nation's troubles were but an advanced state of similar economic and political pressures found in many other BEMs—growth that was too reliant on foreign borrowing, mixed with a government unable to manage the powerful political pressures acting on it at home and abroad. In 1996, when Washington and Beijing went to the brink of a trade war over

China's refusal to enforce laws protecting patents, trademarks, and copyrights—what is called "intellectual property"—it was an acute case of problems similar to those America has with many other BEMs. A few months later when India refused to sign the comprehensive nuclear test ban treaty despite massive U.S. arm-twisting to do so, or when the Turkish prime minister concluded an oil deal with Iran in defiance of American efforts to isolate Iran with sanctions, New Delhi and Ankara were reflecting the growing political independence that the Big Ten are exercising. And when South Korean police brutally stormed several universities to quell rioting in August 1996, or when Indonesian President Suharto repressed political dissent that same month, the seething pressures for more freedom reflected similar, albeit less acute, tensions in other BEMs undergoing tumultuous political and economic change.

Why should Americans care about this group of ten countries? Who are they, and why are they important? Let's take a look at the ten central players in the dramatic global transformation that is underway.

The Big Ten

Mexico

As so many Americans now know from the heated political debates over NAFTA in 1993 and the financial crisis of 1995, Mexico presents both great opportunities and great dilemmas for the United States. A nation of 88 million people, it is the second largest country in all of Latin America and shares a thousand-mile land border with the United States. Our two nations are closely intertwined by trade, investment, banking, legal and illegal movement of people, as well as the need for close cooperation on environmental protection and narcotics trafficking. Mexico represents an enormous commercial market for American firms, but its cheap labor also poses threats to the American workforce, and its history of booms and busts has on more than one occasion created havoc with our economic links. In the late 1990s, Mexico will be preoccupied with recovering from a financial crisis, opening its economy toward greater foreign trade, and moving its political system to more democracy.

Before the peso collapsed in 1995, Mexico was gaining substantial political influence around the world. It was the first developing country in the hemisphere to join the Organization of Economic Cooperation and Development—the "rich nations' club" of the United States, Canada, Australia, Japan, and Western Europe—and the first Latin American country to join the Asian-Pacific Economic Cooperation forum, a Pacific Rim grouping that includes the United States and that seeks to create a free trade zone within the next few decades. To its great credit, Mexico responded to its financial crisis decisively and courageously, resisting severe pressures to erect new trade barriers or to slow down important free market reforms. It has already repaid the emergency loans to the United States that kept it afloat in 1995, and has regained its ability to borrow funds in international markets. Mexico, in fact, is moving from being a very closed economy to one of the most open trading nations. Today, an economic recovery appears on the horizon, and the economic fundamentals look strong. And although the road back will take time to travel, before the end of the century, Mexico is likely to reemerge as a prosperous nation, and one with substantial influence in the hemisphere and beyond. It will also resume its place as one of America's most important markets. Already U.S. exports are back to pre-crisis levels.

Brazil

With 165 million people, Brazil is the largest country in South America in population and also in geographical territory. Charles de Gaulle, former president of France, is rumored to have said, "Brazil is the country of the future . . . and will always be." For Brazil, the future is now. Historically plagued by hyperinflation, sometimes as high as 2,500 percent per year, under its last and current government Brazil has reduced annual price rises to below 15 percent. The economy used to be protected by large tariffs and tight quotas on imports, and some products like computers and cars were kept out completely. All this is ending. There has been substantial trade liberalization and an unprecedented welcoming of foreign investment. Today Brazil accounts for over a quarter of all imports from around the world into Latin America and the Caribbean. It is the single largest destination for American investment in South America, and is our largest trading partner there. The country has a highly advanced technological base, and huge requirements to build a modern infrastructure in such areas as transportation and communication—auguring well for its potential as an ever greater trading partner for the United States.

Brazil is also playing a larger role on the world stage than ever before. It is a strong voice in global trade negotiations, a supporter of nuclear nonproliferation, and a provider of troops for peacekeeping operations. Closer to home, Brasilia is taking the lead in building a South American trading block called Mercosur, which now links the country to Argentina, Uruguay, Paraguay, Bolivia, and Chile, and which could become a rival to NAFTA. Brazil's growing political clout in the hemisphere is tangible. Over the past few years, Washington has worked hard to build cooperative ties with governments from Canada to the tip of Argentina. Before every important policy decision, it has had to get Brazil's consent and agree with Brasilia on the next steps.

Argentina

Until the early 1990s Argentina, like Brazil, was decimated by inflation. It, too, has brought runaway prices under tight control. It has transformed itself from a highly protectionist economy to an open one. Probably no other country in the developing world has moved so extensively to sell its government-owned companies to private investors. Until the Mexico crisis in 1995, which cast an economic shadow across Latin America, Argentina experienced industrial growth that was among the highest in the world, fueled by a rise in investment and productivity. The strength of a nation is judged by many criteria these days, but in an era in which economic and financial policies count for so much, Argentina has impressed the global markets by its ability to withstand a serious recession in 1995 and continue pursuing free market policies. The country has a highly sophisticated industrial and agricultural sector. Despite its relatively small population—35 million—it has become an attractive commercial partner for the United States, not only because of its extensive economic reforms, but also because of its membership in Mercosur. American companies like General Motors or IBM see great opportunities to use Argentina as a base to sell and invest throughout the region. Together, Argentina and Brazil account for over half the Gross Domestic Product (GDP) of Latin America.

South Africa

Across the Atlantic, South Africa, with a population of 41 million, represents over 45 percent of the GDP of its entire continent. It is the most advanced, productive, and balanced economy in all of Africa, not to mention the most vibrant democracy and the most potent military force. It has a modern infrastructure, and highly sophisticated industries in finance, communications, transport, and energy, as well as several home-grown multinational companies. It has one of the most advanced stock exchanges in the world. Its market absorbs products from all of Africa and its companies provide critically essential goods and services for all of its neighboring countries.

Pretoria's success will spill over into all of Africa, as will its failures. A peaceful, democratic, and prosperous South Africa would set a good example of a country that has managed to reconcile and overcome ethnic divisions, whereas a South Africa that fails in this effort would send alarming signals throughout the continent. But in addition to being so influential in its own neighborhood, South Africa could be a powerful trading partner and ally to America because of its future growth potential as well as its ethnic bond with African-Americans.

Turkey

Turkey, with a population of 61 million people, occupies one of the most strategic positions in the world, sharing borders with Syria, Iraq, and Iran, not to mention the Balkans and several countries on the southern flank of the former Soviet Union. It is a member of NATO and has formed a customs union with the European Union. It has long been a military ally of the United States, supplying bases and troops, most recently in the Gulf War. The country has overwhelming importance to America as a strategic ally in a highly volatile Islamic region; indeed, Washington is counting on it to be a bulwark against the spread of Islamic fundamentalism into Europe. Turkey is among the most industrialized nations outside of America, Western Europe, and Japan, and it aspires to be an economic hub for the vast region that surrounds it. Its strong historical and ethnic ties to neighboring countries, as well as its huge market and its commercial expertise, put it in a good position to achieve this goal, provided it gets its own economic house in order with sounder budget policies and privatization of state-owned firms. It is already the largest U.S. trading partner in the region, but the potential is much greater.

Poland

The largest country in Eastern Europe, with 39 million people—more than Hungary and the Czech Republic combined—Poland was the first post-Communist country to emerge from the recession that blanketed the region after the dissolution of the former Soviet Union. Poland quickly established a democracy, moved rapidly to privatize its economy, and made remarkable strides in getting its finances in order. Once a Soviet-style economy dominated by heavy industry, it has moved quickly to build a service-oriented sector based on banking, tourism, health care, and leisure activities. Poland has emerged as the most entrepreneurial country in the ex-Communist region, sprouting some two million new businesses in the 1990s. With one of the fastest growing economies on the continent, it has become the beneficiary of large-scale investment from Europe, particularly from Germany and the United States. It is also emerging as a key trading partner for American firms in a region with a highly educated workforce and the biggest and most stable middle class in the former Soviet bloc. This country, which aspires to join the European Union and NATO and has an excellent chance of doing both, wields a great deal of influence in a region that is now at the heart of a much enlarged Europe.

South Korea

Across the Pacific there are four Asian BEMs. South Korea, with 45 million people, is the most highly industrialized of all of the Big Ten. In the last few decades, Seoul's rapid economic advancement has made South Korea one of the most economically powerful nations outside of North America, Western Europe, and Japan. Its economy represents about 7 percent of the entire East Asian GDP, and its highly protected market, were it to open more quickly, holds great potential for American firms. Between 1994 and 1995, for example, despite its huge trade barriers, both exports and imports of South Korea increased by over 30 percent—more than those of any other major country.

Seoul has become a major foreign investor in Asia, with hundreds of millions of dollars pouring into China, Vietnam, Indonesia, and elsewhere. It is also a fierce competitor, as companies like Samsung or Goldstar have burst onto the global scene in the last decade. In education, as well as research and development, South Korea can match many European nations.

Strategically, South Korea is a crucial partner for the United

States in Northeast Asia, where the North and South Korean armies maintain a state of high readiness to confront one another in what may be the most serious possibility of large-scale war anywhere in the world today. Nevertheless, peaceful reunification of the two Koreas is also a plausible scenario, in which case we may see the emergence of a powerhouse in all dimensions—economic, industrial, and military.

China

With a population of 1.2 billion, China is by far the biggest of the BEMs. By several measures it is likely to be one of the three largest economies within the next decade. Beijing has attracted commitments of overseas funds on the order of $80 billion per year in 1994 and 1995, half of which has already been invested, making it the largest destination of direct foreign investment in the developing world, and the fourth largest in the world behind the United States, Great Britain, and France.

No market holds more long-term potential for America, and China has become a key element in the global strategy of hundreds of America's top firms. The future of China is also the future of most of Asia. If China is able to link its vast economy further into the global network of trade and finance, world commerce could expand significantly. If China can establish itself as a nation seeking peace with all of its neighbors, as well as become a force to help settle regional disputes, then the prospects for Asia are indeed bright. On the other hand, China may prove to be an enormously disruptive force in the region, creating serious military and economic tensions from Seoul to Sydney. It is likely that our relationship with China will emerge in the next decade as the most important focus of our entire foreign policy.

Not only is China itself a big emerging market, but so is the "Chinese Economic Area" comprising China, Hong Kong, and Taiwan. Hong Kong, after all, will become part of China in the summer of 1997. And despite political tensions, commercial ties between Beijing and Taipei are booming. Taiwanese investors have had a heavy focus on low-technology production of such items as shoes and toys. Now, however, they are moving into more sophisticated products such as Chinese-languages computer software and biotechnology. Many innovative companies already see the Chinese Economic Area as an integrated market. From the outset the Clinton administration called the Chinese Economic Area a BEM, rather than just China.

Indonesia

Indonesia, with a population of 194 million, is the world's fourth largest nation in terms of people, and the world's largest Muslim nation. It has become not just one of the world's fastest-growing countries but also the home to billions of dollars of American investment, particularly in the energy sector, but increasingly also in manufacturing. Indonesia has also been a regular supplier of peacekeeping forces around the world.

Like many other BEMs, the significance of Indonesia to American interests can be accurately gauged only by looking at its role and influence in its wider region. And in Southeast Asia, Indonesia is both a major economic and military force. It plays a leading role in the important Association of Southeast Asian Nations (ASEAN), a group comprised of several very rapidly growing countries including Thailand, Malaysia, and Vietnam, and one that is now beginning to coordinate its trade and military policies and is becoming an integrated market with a population of 414 million and a combined GDP of over $500 billion. In fact, the real BEM is not just Indonesia, but ASEAN itself; this actually was how the Clinton administration ultimately defined the BEM in the region. This broader interpretation of a big emerging market in Southeast Asia makes good sense, because American companies are seeing it the same way—linking themselves through trade and investment to one or another of the countries, often with the idea of using them as a platform to serve the entire ASEAN market.

Indonesia is important to the United States for another reason. With China, it is the only BEM without a democratic foundation. The pressures for a more open political society are building, creating great tensions which could burst into a crisis for the country, the region, and the international financial system.

India

India, with a population of 914 million, including a "middle class" of well over 100 million people, is vast by any standard. It has a diversified industrial base, with large-scale production of coal, steel, cement, chemicals, heavy machinery, and textiles. Its highly trained and educated workforce has helped make it one of the world's largest exporters of computer software.

Unlike many BEMs, India has a sophisticated commercial and legal code. Like the others, it has placed economic progress at the heart of its national policies, and in just the last few years it has succeeded in opening its economy to the rest of the world beyond anything that most observers would have imagined possible in so short a time. Between 1991 and 1995, the government largely abolished a heavy-handed system in which anyone wanting to set up a business needed to struggle through months, if not years, of red tape to get a license; it slashed tariffs from a maximum of 300 percent to 50 percent; it ended government monopolies in electric power, telecommunications, and aviation; and it welcomed foreign investment for the first time in fifty years.

The United States is already India's largest economic partner, and its trade and investment links with America are sure to grow. Like China, India has a nuclear weapons capability, a large army, and an aspiring navy, guaranteeing it influence well beyond economics. India and its neighbor, Pakistan, have clashed three times since independence in 1947, and continued military tensions among those two potential nuclear powers make the region one of the world's most dangerous hotspots.

The Selection Criteria

It is never easy to select some countries and reject others. No two countries are alike, so many criteria must be weighed. In identifying the BEMs, here are some of the key considerations used in selecting which countries qualify:

They have large populations, large resource bases, large markets, and are powerhouses in their respective regions. China, India, and Indonesia are three of the four most populous countries in the world. Each of these, plus Brazil, occupy enormous land masses. If any of the Big Ten are economically successful, their progress will spur development in the countries all around them. Conversely, if they experience an economic crisis, they have the capacity to bring down their neighbors.

They are bursting onto the world scene, shattering the status quo. With the Cold War over, the big emerging markets are seeking their place in the global hierarchy. They are finding a new sense of national pride. They want a larger voice in international politics. They want a bigger share of the global economic pie. In order to build their economies and to enhance their global competitiveness and prestige, they want to acquire the latest technology and put it to work effectively. Their young workers will produce hundreds of billions of dollars worth of products that will be less expensive than ours, and often just as good. This will cause major changes in the structure of world trade and investment, painful dislocations for millions of American workers, and strong downward pressure on American wages.

They are critical participants in the major political, economic, and social dramas taking place on the world scene. All the BEMs are struggling to make the transition from authoritarian state-run economies to democratic capitalism, and on their success rests the future of global politics and economics. The three Latin-American BEMs will determine whether the entire continent can escape the recurrent boom-and-bust cycles of the last century.

The four Asian BEMs will determine whether East Asia will be characterized by expanding trade and investment and stunning economic progress, or whether it will descend into the political and military rivalries more characteristic of Europe in the first half of this century. India will be the most significant test case for whether democracy and capitalism can deal effectively with mass poverty. Turkey is the wall that could stop Islamic fundamentalism from reaching well into Europe. South Africa will show whether racial harmony and democratic capitalism can coexist.

They are the world's fastest expanding markets, and responsible for a good deal of the world's explosive growth of trade. The United States now exports more in goods and services to the ten big emerging markets than to all of Europe and Japan combined. Over the next decade, East Asia alone will account for almost half of all growth in the purchase of cars, telecommunications equipment, and movies. The ten countries are all moving quickly up the ladder of economic development, educating their populations, training their workforces, expanding technical research, building modern infrastructures.

They are all trying to open their economies, balance their budgets, and sell off their state companies. All but two have instituted substantial political liberalization. The pace of economic opening in Argentina, India, and Poland has startled most experts. The opening of political systems in Brazil, South Africa, and South Korea is also impressive. But not all of the BEMs have made good on the promise of capitalism and democracy, and where this hasn't happened there are offsetting factors of overwhelming commercial or strategic importance to the United States that still compel their inclusion in the BEM category. For example, China and Indonesia have made significant economic strides, even though Beijing remains a Communist government and Jakarta is a powerful autocracy. However, their markets are critical for us, as are their political stability and the dampening of any expansionist ambitions they may have. Turkey's economic policies have floundered, but it is a vibrant democracy, and Ankara's strategic position is too important for us to ignore.

While ten countries do stand out, this is not a static number. The ten should be considered representative of a category of country. During the Commerce Department's examination of the BEMs, several countries were heatedly discussed but ultimately rejected from this category. For example, in the original selection, the most controversial decision was to exclude Russia. After all, it was big, powerful, and would surely rate high on America's radar screen for years to come. Ultimately, we chose not to put Moscow on the list. It was not far enough along with its economic reforms, its political leadership seemed too precarious, and consequently the prospects for progress were simply too uncertain. Also, because of its enormous military and nuclear capability, Russia belonged in a category by itself and was already getting an enormous amount of high-level attention in Washington.

In selecting India, we also considered Pakistan, but it carried nowhere near the global influence of its southern neighbor. And although it has made some impressive economic reforms, the potential of Pakistan's market appeared much less than that of India's. In focusing on Indonesia, Thailand also arose as a candidate. That was a close call, but Indonesia carried much more weight on the global scene. Ultimately, moreover, it made sense to think of Indonesia as the hub of the ASEAN region, which would, in any event, include Thailand.

When we were looking at Argentina, Venezuela also popped up on our screen. But whereas Buenos Aires had taken the hard economic decisions toward economic reform, Caracas's policies were in a total shambles, with little prospect, in our view at the time, that they would improve. On more than one occasion, representatives of the Greek government admonished us for having included Turkey and not Greece. Although the two countries have been rivals, we did not ascribe to them the same geopolitical significance.

Why BEMs Matter—A Tale of
Two Very Different Futures

The starting point for a discussion of why BEMs really matter to the United States is the range of changes that are occurring in the international arena and in the BEMs themselves, and the relationship between the two.

As we all know, the end of the Cold War brought a dramatic decline of global military tensions and a parallel increase in our focus on our everyday lives, including our schools, health care, pensions, and crime. These preoccupations coincided with increasing trade and foreign investment around the world, such that it has become difficult to divorce our future from the state of the world economy.

Even for the United States, despite its size and strength, the global links have been increasingly critical. Over the last four years, our exports have grown about three times as fast as the overall economy, and our sales to foreign countries have accounted for about a third of our economic growth. Today exports support about 11 million jobs, which typically pay some 15 percent more than the manufacturing wage, and which are more resistant than others to downsizing and recession. Exports will be even more important in the future. Over the last twenty-five years, trade as a percentage of our economic activity (GDP) has grown from 11 percent to 23 percent, and the trend is straight up. By the year 2000, over 16 million jobs are likely to depend on exports, and nearly 30 percent of America's GDP may involve trade. A similar story could be told about the importance of our imports, how dependent we have become on oil or certain electrical components, how foreign goods stimulate competition in our country and help hold down inflation, how much our everyday choices are expanded by the enormous volume of foreign-made products available to us. Or we could look at the hundreds of billions of dollars that America borrows from other countries to help service our debts while keeping interest rates lower than they would be if all our borrowing had to be drawn solely from the savings of Americans.

International linkages are growing because of the dramatic expansion of capitalism and democracy abroad. But the simultaneous blossoming of more open politics and more open economies has created a very uncertain environment to which our fate is being hitched. On the one hand, it is plausible to believe that we are entering a golden age in which businesses will join hands across borders, barriers to international commerce will fall, modern technology will spread everywhere, and economic growth around the world will soar. On the other hand, new democracies tend to be chaotic, because they do not have the underlying foundations—a history of elections, the presence of a skilled government bureaucracy to provide efficient services without corruption, or an effective judicial system—that give mature democracies stability. And countries opening their markets for the first time create another form of chaos, as government controls are lifted and business experiences a free-for-all without sound regulations or other established rules of the game. On top of this simultaneous political and business chaos is the fact that newly freed people demand more from their governments than can possibly be delivered, leading to widespread popular disillusionment and a backlash against both democracy and free markets.

We can therefore envision two different futures. In the first, capitalism and democracy flourish, even if there are some ups and downs along the way. Some countries take two steps forward and one back, but the favorable trends persist, and with them comes an age of unprecedented prosperity. A second scenario, however, is that political and economic chaos leads to a return to authoritarianism and government-controlled economies, including a sharp rise in trade protectionism. This would happen if large segments of the population in many nations experiencing democracy and free markets for the first time conclude that this form of capitalism is not working for them, that lots of people are getting rich but many more are mired in misery, and that the Darwinian environment is too painful and not politically acceptable.

Obviously, the United States has an enormous stake in which scenario materializes. We will gain enormously from a steady increase in democratic capitalism, not only because trade will increase but also because the environment will be more peaceful and there will be less need for U.S. military intervention. But if the second scenario comes to pass, our economic interests will suffer greatly, global political tensions will mushroom, and we could be drawn into foreign conflicts as governments return to the tradition of building up their armies as a diversion from their domestic problems.

The ten big emerging markets stand in the middle of all these currents. That is why they are so important to the global scene, and to the United States in particular. As a group, the BEMs hold the key to the steady expansion of global trade and investment and to the evolution of democracy. They are, after all, the territories where large-scale experiments in creating open political and economic systems are taking place. Their size and power make what happens within their borders, and between them and other countries, of global significance. If they succeed, we all do. If they fail, then they will have thrown a gigantic monkey wrench into the wheel of global economic and political progress.

The Big Emerging Markets: As Important as Europe and Japan

It is precisely because of their pivotal role in the international arena that the importance of the big emerging markets must be reweighed in the total calculus of American interests. For a century we have been preoccupied with Western Europe and Japan. This is understandable given the history and culture we share with much of Europe, the important alliances that we have had, the personal friendships that have been built up, and the fact that the overwhelming bulk of our commercial relations has historically been with these industrialized nations. Although the glue that has bound us together is sure to loosen now that we do not have the Soviet Union as a common enemy, it will be of great importance that we maintain these ties. But a true assessment of our future interests would compel at least as much attention to the BEMs—which would mean a sea change in our foreign policy .

Indeed, if we make a cold-eyed assessment of where our future priorities lie, we would conclude that the world's dynamism is unlikely to be found in Europe or Japan, but instead in the Big Ten. Our global commercial interests, so important in this era, will be expanding in the big emerging markets to a much greater degree than in Europe and Japan, if for no other reason than that the BEMs will be growing much faster and our trade and investment will be starting from a much smaller base. But beyond commercial stakes, there is the question of partnering with countries that share America's political and economic energy. For the foreseeable future, that means the BEMs.

Europe is sure to be preoccupied with a broad range of issues that are fundamentally focused inward: building technical and bureaucratic arrangements for enlarging the European Union, creating a common currency, dismantling large-scale social welfare systems, dealing with enormous problems of youth unemployment, and coming to grips with the need to rejuvenate European technological capabilities, which have lagged so far behind those of the U.S. and Japan. As for Japan, no one should discount the possibility that it will reemerge from its long recession and its huge banking problems to become economically vibrant again. But the Japanese economy is still mired in heavy innovation-stifling regulation that, judging from the past pace of reform, is likely to take at least another decade to dismantle. And Japanese internal politics is still in the throes of a very slow transition to a modern democracy, making it incapable of facilitating any dramatic changes in Japanese society.

The lack of vitality in Europe and Japan stand in direct contrast to the rapidly changing character of American society—our entrepreneurism, our technological capabilities, and our political laboratory, which allows fifty state governments to experiment with new approaches to governing. There is nothing static about the United States; in fact, we are still a revolutionary society. We are also a multicultural nation, becoming even more so with immigration from Asia and Latin America—a situation that is likely to shift the weight of attention of the American people away from Europe and Japan to countries like Mexico, Brazil, China, India, South Korea, and the ASEAN region. In this respect, in the future we are likely to have at least as much in common with many of the Big Ten as with our historic trading and military partners. We will certainly have much more in common with them in the emerging global arena than ever before in history.

The following chapters will discuss the full ramifications of engagement with the big emerging markets—the opportunities, the risks, the new imperatives for America. For now, here is a snapshot of the factors that will make them important to our future:

- The big emerging markets will be a powerful force propelling economic growth around the world. If most nations continue to open their economies to trade, and if the BEMs continue their trend of sound economic policies, then the Big Ten will grow two to three times as fast as the United States and the other major industrialized countries over the next decade. The compounding effect will be dramatic.

- Already the United States exports more to the BEMs than to Japan and Western Europe. But if current trends continue, the Commerce Department estimates that the BEMs will account for $1 trillion in incremental American exports between 1990 and 2010.

- The future of world trade depends on the BEMs. Because of the growing needs of their consumers, hundreds of millions of whom are now entering the middle class, and because they will require hundreds of billions of dollars of imports to build transportation, telecommunications, and energy-generating facilities, the Big Ten will provide an enormous proportion of the incremental increase in world trade.

- But it is not just the dollar value of trade that is at issue. The trade *policies* of the BEMs will determine whether we have a truly open trading system, or whether it veers toward new forms of protectionism and compartmentalization. The outcome depends in large part on whether China joins the World Trade Organization and agrees to trade by globally accepted rules, whether India opens its economy further to foreign investors, whether South Korea follows the old, protectionist Japan model or the more free-market American example, whether Argentina agrees to tighter control over protection of intellectual property rights—and a host of similar issues in other BEMs.

- The big emerging markets will have a major impact on the industrial structure of the world and the United States. Not only will they provide enormous markets for our products, but they will also supply an unprecedented number of productive, low-paid workers to the world market. A reasonable estimate is that over 1 billion people, mostly from the BEMs, will enter the global economy in the next ten years. They'll earn, say, $5 to $10 per day, compared to $80 to $90 that their U.S. counterparts will earn. With the diffusion of technology and the injection of Western or Japanese management techniques, they could be 85 percent as efficient as workers in the West. For America, the implications for commercial competition, employment, wages, the cohesion of communities, politics—virtually everything—are staggering.

- The size of the markets in the Big Ten will create brutal rivalries among American, Japanese, and European companies, all assisted by their own governments, who will provide low-cost financing or political pressure on Ankara, or Pretoria, or Brasilia. Already the BEMs are becoming major wedges in the trade and diplomatic ties between America and other industrialized nations.

- Geopolitics will increasingly revolve around the Big Ten. Their growing economic weight will be felt in the governing councils of major international institutions of growing importance such as the International Monetary Fund and the World Trade Organization. Some of the big emerging markets will be pivotal to the resolution of key conflicts between China and Taiwan, the two Koreas, and India and Pakistan.

- The very nature of global politics will change as tensions within countries become as internationally significant as those between them. Bosnia was a civil war, compelling U.S. involvement. If the economies of South Africa, Turkey, Mexico, or Indonesia were to go into reverse gear, and if there were major civil strife, the dilemmas for Washington would be excruciating. Not only could there be bloodshed, but unlike Bosnia, there could be serious repercussions to the global financial system.

- The world's ability to make progress on a host of global issues depends on active cooperation of the BEMs—China and Indonesia on human rights; Mexico and Turkey on narcotics; China and Brazil on the environment—to cite but a few examples.

- ***Most important of all: The ability of the world to move toward a democratic-capitalist society, where individuals have dignity, where freedom is the rule, and where living standards rise for all, depends on the simultaneous economic and political openings occurring in all the BEMs.***

In short, there are powerful new forces in the world, and the BEMs are at the crux of all of them. These new realities are the reason we need a careful assessment of our interests in the Big Ten, and why we must adopt a new way of thinking about our role and our priorities in the world.

2 | The Rewards of Economic Engagement

The opportunities for American firms and American investors in the BEMs derive in large part from the healthy growth prospects of the Big Ten, who are projected to grow two to three times as fast as the United States, Europe, and Japan.

Our exports to the Big Ten are climbing rapidly; U.S. financial investors are expanding their involvement in the BEMs; and U.S. businesses are gearing their global strategy to these markets.

There are good reasons to believe these trends can continue.

THE FIRST IN-DEPTH STUDY that the Department of Commerce did on a single big emerging market concerned Indonesia. It was the summer of 1993, and for the first time that any of my Commerce colleagues could remember, all the resources of the U.S. government had been brought to bear on the question: What was the totality of our commercial interests in Indonesia? What were the export prospects, what opportunities did U.S. firms have to invest, what hurdles needed to be overcome, what would the competition be like?

The analysis was detailed, identifying not only particular sectors but also specific projects. We marshaled information from all the traditional sources, such as the State Department and the Export-Import Bank, and also from more specialized agencies like the Department of Transportation and the Bureau of Mines at the Interior Department. I personally took a draft of the study with me on a trip to Jakarta so our ambassador and his staff could review, critique, and modify it. On that same trip, I met with the heads of U.S. companies operating in the country to complete our report with the most timely, on-the-ground information. What stands out in my mind, nearly four years later, is how surprised we all were about the sum total of the commercial opportunities in the next decade alone—which amounted to some $50 billion dollars in potential sales—beyond the traditional U.S. involvement in the energy sector. What I also remember is that America's overall economic position in Indonesia was slipping and that European, Japanese, and other Asian nations were grabbing an increasing proportion of market share. We were determined to redouble our export promotion efforts, and we did.

———

Not long ago, many people would have looked at international trade and finance through lenses other than those of the big emerging markets. During the late 1980s and early 1990s, Americans were preoccupied with Japan and Germany as the two countries around which most of the big global economic issues would revolve. I myself was part of the crowd. In a book entitled *A Cold Peace: America, Japan, Germany, and the Struggle for Supremacy*, I predicted that the great opportunities and the great commercial struggles in the coming years would hinge on relationships among these three powers, primarily on how competition among the three would be managed, and how savvy government leaders were in managing their common economic interests. In his presidential campaign of 1992, Bill Clinton talked regularly about the primacy of economics in America's domestic and foreign policy—and he almost always used Japan and Germany as the symbols of the challenges ahead.

In fact, we were all fighting the last war rather than the next one. Even as *A Cold Peace* was being put to bed in the spring of 1992, I already had an uneasy feeling of having missed many of the new trends in trade and finance. The buzz on Wall Street about emerging markets was getting louder. And as I toured the country that summer to promote the book, my audiences were extremely interested in what Tokyo and Bonn were doing, but the second or third question was always, "What about Mexico?" or "What about China?" The public was ahead of me, and ahead of most of the other "experts" as well.

Economic Growth Is the Critical Factor

What so many of us underestimated were the powerful growth patterns in Asia, the strength of the recovery in Latin America from the decade-long debt crisis, and the rapidity with which Eastern Europe would move toward capitalism.

Indeed, most of the power which big emerging markets are now gathering results from the economic growth that has occurred in the last few years. Many of the basic policies necessary to continue that growth have been put in place. The situations of individual BEMs varies widely, but all are trying to move in the same direction—reining in budget deficits, controlling inflation, reducing government ownership of industries, and opening up their economies to international trade. And everywhere there is a keen desire to join the world economy and reap maximum benefits from it. Adam Smith has won a decisive victory over Karl Marx.

It is difficult to exaggerate how dramatic a change this is for most of the Big Ten. As recently as the late 1980s, Latin America was mired in debt, recession, and runaway inflation. I saw the problem firsthand in the 1980s as an investment banker advising Latin American governments and firms. I remember, in particular, spending several months on and off in Brazil, watching one foreign firm after another close down operations, meeting with Brazilian businesspeople who were starved for credit, and hearing my colleagues on Wall Street say that the country was "finished." Just a few years ago, South Africa was still a siege state, dominated by a small minority using near-totalitarian controls. Poland was in the grip of communism, its economy in shambles. Turkey was an economic disaster for a good deal of the 1980s. China, even though still a communist state in political terms, had taken but the first steps toward economic reform. Only the nations of Southeast Asia were moving to a free-market rhythm, albeit one that was much less forceful than today.

The turnarounds have been spectacular. Argentina brought inflation down from over 2,000 percent per year in 1989 to under 5 percent today. Brazil's progress was nearly as dramatic. Mexico has demonstrated that it can weather a severe financial crisis and still continue to open its economy to trade and foreign investment—in direct contrast to the way it handled previous crises by raising tariffs, blocking foreign companies from coming in, and nationalizing whole sectors like banking. India has opened its economy to the world for the first time since independence; it has attracted more foreign investment in the last three years than in the past forty-five combined. Poland has become the fastest-growing economy in Europe. China, once closed to the world, will soon become one of the top six trading nations. The Association of South East Asian Nations (ASEAN) is becoming a gigantic free-trade region with a combined GDP of over $500 billion.

Growth in the big emerging markets will produce dramatic changes in the global economy, including a shift of wealth and power. In 1995 these countries accounted for 10.2 percent of the world's economic output. In less than two decades that share is likely to double. Not long ago, the Organization for Economic Cooperation and Development (OECD) projected that if China, India, and Indonesia each grew by 6 percent per year for the next fifteen years—well within existing trends—700 million people in these countries would then have an average income equal to that of the average Spaniard today. Seven hundred million people is equivalent to the combined populations of America, Japan, and Western Europe.

The prospects for East Asia outside Japan are particularly bright, even though the economic miracle may slow in the short term. Over the last decade, economic growth in this region, excluding Japan, averaged 8.5 percent, four times the rate of the West. Projections show that the GDP of East Asia is set to double every decade even at slightly lower growth rates.

Again, while any projections about the future need to be hedged, they should be seen in an historical context: It took Great Britain fifty-eight years to double its national income during the Industrial Revolution. It took the United States forty-seven years to do the same beginning with industrial takeoff in the mid-1800s. It took Japan thirty-four years in the late 1800s. It took South Korea eleven years in the late 1960s. And today China is doing it faster than any of these countries did. An open world economy, including the availability of money and technology from all over the globe, has made this spectacular growth pattern possible.

This growth is not merely of interest to economists; it is the key to so much of what is happening in the global arena. It is why our sales to the big emerging markets are booming. It is why political agitation within these countries has been contained so far, even as income inequality rises and social tensions grow (although we should worry about the future, as we will see later). The spectacular economic expansion in these markets is also crucial to our own growth. America's economy is now highly dependent on trade for its own expansion. In the future, exports represent one of the most promising areas to increase our modest growth trajectory. Moreover, it used to be that when the major industrial countries went into a slump, the entire world would follow. This is not the case now. Despite slower economic growth in the United States, Europe, and Japan, the big emerging markets have continued their expansion at a brisk pace. That's good news, for it means that there are sources of economic stimulus in the world other than our traditional trading partners on which we can rely.

Why Growth Is Likely to Continue

A lot can happen to throw current trends off track—depressions, political instability, wars. But barring such events and conditions, it is likely that robust growth will continue in the big emerging markets for a number of reasons:

BEMs have the right mind-set. The global economic *gestalt* is very favorable. The entire world is hooked on an effort to attract more foreign money, technology, and skilled manpower. Today, countries are competing to see who can move the fastest to balance budgets, bring inflation down, and maintain steady exchange rates, and those in the lead are rewarded by their ability to attract foreign investment. This competition is the exact opposite of the protectionism of the 1930s, when nations rushed to beat one another to erect barriers to imports and to devalue their currencies in order to make their products excessively cheap in world markets.

Another positive element in the behavior of emerging market leaders is the willingness to move ahead with trade liberalization. It is not very long since protectionist ideas were fashionable. In Latin America, the buzz word used to be "import substitution"—keeping imports out and building domestic industries with subsidies. In Asia, the Japanese style of "industrial policy," in which the government promoted exports but kept out foreign products, was also in vogue.

In the last few years, however, these mind-sets have changed. The North American Free Trade Agreement (NAFTA), linking the United States, Canadian, and Mexican markets, was concluded. The most ambitious round of global trade liberalization ever undertaken was wrapped up, and with it a new and powerful institution, the World Trade Organization (WTO), was established with full participation from most of the Big Ten. (China, not a member of the WTO's predecessor, the General Agreement on Tariffs and Trade, or GATT, was an observer at the negotiations.) The nations of Mercosur and ASEAN agreed to drop trade barriers among themselves, and on a broader scale, the Asian Pacific Economic Co-operation forum (APEC), comprised of eighteen countries ranging from Japan and China to the United States and Mexico, agreed to achieve free trade among their members over the next twenty-five years.

The BEMs have little choice but to be economically disciplined. Another reason to be optimistic about continued economic progress is that both internal and external pressures leave the BEMs with little choice but to stay on course with free market policies. It is possible to envision these trends being slowed, or even halted for a while. However, unless there is a global economic catastrophe, or unless governments totally falter, it is difficult to conceive of the momentum being reversed. At the same time that economic freedom has been creating powerful middle classes in these countries, the prospect of political freedom has given these same people a mechanism to hold their governments more accountable for pursuing policies that lift living standards.

At the same time, outside forces allow the big emerging markets little leeway to diverge from free market policies without serious adverse consequences. The global market would clobber them if they did. As the *New York Times* columnist Thomas L. Friedman likes to say, there are two superpowers these days: the United States and Moody's bond rating service. In an instant, Moody's can downgrade the credit of a misbehaving emerging market, causing funds to flow out and sending the country into a tailspin. The fact is that none of the Big Ten can achieve its goals now without significant and consistent infusions of capital. And the providers of that money are looking for the right policies to be proclaimed and implemented. Global investors will pull the plug at a moment's notice. No one dares to call their bluff, particularly after Wall Street forced Mexico to its knees when its policies went astray in 1994.

The economic fundamentals look good. In Asia the fundamentals are particularly impressive. Savings rates are the highest in the world, reaching 30 to 35 percent of national income, compared to under 5 percent in the United States. Investment is soaring in education, research, airports, and telephone systems. Fiscal policies are tight, central banks are conservative, and individual initiative is stressed.

Latin America lags behind Asia, but from Mexico to Argentina and Chile, there is cause for optimism because policies are moving in a better direction than at any time in the last quarter century. The selling off of state-owned companies is proceeding, and the climate for private investors is improving. There is substantial experimentation, such as Chile's willingness to let workers invest their own social security funds, which reflects a sophisticated understanding of markets. Moreover, the Latin American region has been tested by fire and proved it can handle the heat. When the Mexican economy went from boom to bust overnight, in the winter of 1994–95, a large number of experts looking at Brazil and Argentina would have predicted that both would be caught in the crisis as they had been when Mexico defaulted on its debt in 1982, kicking off a series of debt defaults across Latin America. They were all wrong.

The BEMs have huge untapped potential. We've seen only the first stage of the big emerging markets' growth. Because they are big, there is enormous scope to expand domestically and regionally. In most of the Big Ten, economic progress has been propelled by foreign trade and investment, much of it limited to large cities and selected regions. China's expansion is overwhelmingly centered on the southern coast. In Brazil, the state of São Paulo preempts most of the new investment and economic growth of the entire country. In Indonesia, nearly all the modern business infrastructure is in Jakarta and nearby surroundings. Therefore, the opportunity to expand into the "hinterlands" is nearly unlimited for the next several decades.

In addition, most of the big emerging markets' trade historically has been with industrial countries. This stems from either old colonial relationships or from links with the multinational corporations of America, Japan, and Europe. It is also the result of years of protectionism and state domination that blocked imports from other developing countries that were competitive in the same products. Enormous changes are afoot which will stimulate more trade with new partners and more investment in production, marketing, technology, and workers. In East Asia, intra-Asian trade is now on the same level as trade across the Pacific and is likely to grow much faster as Asian nations reduce their trade barriers and take advantage of one another's prosperity. The same phenomenon can be seen in the trading pattern of Mercosur in South America.

There is also significant untapped technological promise. Today the Big Ten operate well below the cutting edge of technology. They buy existing technology "off the shelf," but this will not always be the case. Measured as a percentage of GDP, for example, Taiwan and South Korea spend as much on research and development as do most European countries. For other ASEAN nations like Thailand and Singapore, the rate of growth of investment in R&D surpasses that of virtually all industrial countries. No one should be surprised when breakthroughs eventually come from big emerging markets, propelling their economies and their global competitiveness.

Like most countries that are underdeveloped, the BEMs can make major strides in the output of each worker. In this regard, Singapore, a member of the ASEAN group, is leading the way as it focuses intently on getting a higher level of productivity from every employee, no matter what the business. Applying new technology, experimenting with new kinds of distribution systems, expanding training and education programs—nothing is off limits. And while Singapore, a city-state of only 2.5 million people, is much more manageable than South Korea or Mexico, it is an indication of where productivity trends are headed.

American Trade Interests

THE IMPORTANCE OF EXPORTING

Before discussing the exceptional prospects for the sales of American goods in the BEMs, it's worth posing the question, "So why are exports so important?" Some of the answers are well known, some not so obvious. Exports propel our own growth; in the 1990s they have accounted for about a third of the expansion of our GDP. Exports support or create better jobs; studies show that the average export-related job pays about 15 percent more than the average manufacturing job, carries significantly higher benefits, and is less likely to be eliminated in economic downturns than other types of employment. But there are other reasons why exporting has become crucial to the competitiveness of U.S. firms in the evolving world economy.

At a time when competition is so fierce, a company that has a global market can spread its fixed costs more broadly than if it operated only in the United States. A company that exports has diversified its markets, thereby helping to reduce its risks should economic conditions at home deteriorate. Because firms that export are in better touch with consumers around the world, they are channels of information to changing tastes and trends abroad, and are in a position to transmit this information back to the United States, giving American citizens the benefit of more choices in terms of what they can buy.

Exports are also essential to keep American companies competitively sharp. Because we live in a global market, the test of a competitive firm is its level of success around the world. A company that cannot make it in Europe or Japan not only risks losing out to other U.S. corporations that can, but it will also be challenged by foreign companies that operate successfully in their home markets and in ours. Put another way, exports are becoming essential to enhance a company's competitive "timbre."

BEMS: THE WORLD'S MOST DYNAMIC IMPORTERS

For the United States, Western Europe, and Japan, the front line of daily interaction with the big emerging markets is trade. Two-way commerce between the advanced industrial countries and the Big Ten has been soaring. In fact, the BEMs have become a motor force of world trade, absorbing an enormous amount of global exports and supplying ever-increasing amounts of the products we buy.

Today the sales of products and services between the industrialized nations of North America, Europe, and Japan on one hand, and Latin America and Asia on the other, are growing twice as fast as trade among America, Europe, and Japan. In 1990, the emerging markets sold about as much as they bought from the United States, Europe, and Japan combined. By 1995, however, they were importing about $150 billion more than they exported each year, resulting in large trade deficits with the rich countries, and thereby helping us to grow faster. These numbers are bound to fluctuate from year to year, and there will be many cases—such as China's large trade surplus with the United States—that go against the overall trend.

From 1990 to 1994, American exports to emerging markets grew five times as fast as exports to traditional markets. As of 1996, the United States exported more to the big emerging markets than to Western Europe and Japan combined, both of which also export more to emerging markets than they do to their traditional industrial partners. A decade ago, for example, the value of American exports to the ASEAN region was $9.95 billion; today it is over $40 billion. Since 1989, U.S. exports to Argentina have quadrupled, exports to Indonesia have tripled, and exports to India have increased by more than 50 percent. Indeed, given the strong role that exports have played in U.S. economic growth these past several years, the Big Ten are now important enough to us that their continued economic openness has become a matter of the highest national importance.

Between 1995 and 2000 the big emerging markets are projected to increase their imports from all parts of the world by 75 percent, twice the increase projected for the industrialized nations. In fact, the net increase in imports of American goods by big emerging markets between 1990 and 2010 could be over $1 trillion, and that doesn't count their purchases of banking, engineering, or legal services. Commerce Department projections show that by the year 2000 American exports to Indonesia will grow from $29 billion to $97 billion, to South Korea from $84 billion to $236 billion, to South Africa from $20 billion to $36 billion, to India from $24 billion to $79 billion.

The sheer numbers are daunting. Over a billion new consumers, mostly young, will be entering the global economy from emerging markets. They will need everything—cars, airplanes, roads, ports, airports, telephones, satellites, energy generation and transmission, hospitals, medical equipment, pharmaceuticals, and every kind of consumer product. As the Big Ten grow, and as their middle classes expand, their needs will be matched by increasing purchasing power, and they will be able to buy more from us. There will be large-scale requirements for equipment to build the physical infrastructure for modern societies. In East Asia, countries anticipate spending well over a trillion dollars over the next decade alone. The World Bank estimates that Latin America will require $1 billion per week to meet just its needs for electricity, water, sewage systems, ports, airports, and railways.

BIG EMERGING SECTORS

In the Commerce Department we identified several "big emerging *sectors*" as guideposts to where the most lucrative export opportunities for American firms would be. They included information technology (computers, software, and telecommunications equipment); transportation systems (aircraft, autos, airport infrastructure); the health care industry (medical equipment); environmental technology; and the energy industry. Our conclusion was that

American exports in these industries would show astounding growth both because of demand in the Big Ten and American comparative advantage in terms of expertise and quality. In environmental technology the growth in Asian demand (not including Japan) was projected at 17 percent per year between 1992 and 1997; in Latin America, 11.4 percent. The Big Ten were expected to account for over two-thirds of global growth in the power generating equipment market, and for over 70 percent of new prospects for U.S. manufacturers of cars and parts. They would be the world's fastest growing markets for medical devices, amounting to a doubling of projected American exports over the next fifteen years.

THE BENEFITS OF IMPORTING

As we will see, imports from the BEMs into the United States are going to increase substantially. Under the pressure of having to earn the money to pay for all they need to buy from the rest of the world, the industries of the Big Ten will become increasingly competitive with ours, and not just on the low end. From steel to computer chips, from auto parts to machine tools, the BEMs are climbing the ladder of quality and sophistication.

No one should deny that imports can and will cause serious dislocations for many Americans. But the benefits to the United States of importing are enormous. As individuals we gain from lower costs and greater variety on the shelves and in the showrooms. Imports create essential competition for our automobile companies, our aircraft manufacturers, our electronics firms, our banks—nearly every part of our business sector.

Imports also hold down the general levels of our prices, contributing greatly to the low inflation we enjoy. Steady prices are always a boon, but as more Americans retire and live on fixed incomes, low inflation will be more critical than ever to our well-being.

In addition, most American companies that export are also major importers. They are competitive in large part because they have sourced the best components from around the world.

FINANCE

America's economic interaction with the big emerging markets goes well beyond traditional trade. The financial linkages are also growing.

As the world economy becomes more open, Americans are investing more of their cash abroad. In 1995, Americans owned a greater value of foreign stocks than foreigners owned of U.S. stocks for the first time in this century. Roughly 70 percent of these U.S. holdings had been accumulated since 1990. Approximately 14 percent of U.S. holdings of foreign equities, or $50 billion, was invested in emerging markets. Some estimates show that $300 to $325 billion from the United States alone could move into foreign stocks by the year 2000, with 25 percent of this, or over $70 billion, going to emerging markets.

Any projections of this kind are highly speculative, but what is certain is that the amounts of U.S. investment going to emerging markets will grow significantly. For one thing, the size of emerging stock markets is growing very rapidly. Since the mid-1980s, the value of company shares on these markets has increased by more than 300 percent. As more state-owned companies in big emerging markets are sold to private investors, the opportunities for Americans to buy new securities will mushroom. Moreover, although all emerging markets together account for 40 percent of global production, they still represent only 15 percent of global stock market value, so there is a long way to go.

Several trends will converge to make investors in America and elsewhere in the advanced economies more linked to—and more dependent on—emerging markets. For most BEMs, stock market operations have been primitive by American standards. Regulations have been lacking or outmoded, there has been inadequate disclosure of what was being traded and by whom, and enforcement of the laws has been spotty. From Shanghai to São Paulo, the entire regulatory framework for investing is improving as new rules are instituted, often with advice from major investment banks, the New York Stock Exchange, and international regulatory experts.

As a result, pension funds, insurance companies, mutual funds, and other big institutional investors will be increasing their bets in these stock markets. The momentum to invest in the BEMs will accelerate as the aging populations in America, Europe, and Japan desperately search for higher returns for their retirement funds. In the industrialized nations, spending on public pensions is projected to increase from 8 percent of GDP in 1990 to 12 percent in 2010 and well over 17 percent by 2030. This translates into trillions of incremental dollars. Institutional and individual investors will be compelled to look to emerging markets because they will be seeking the higher financial returns that are possible in countries where growth is so strong, and they will be attracted by the perceived added safety that comes with putting their eggs in many baskets. In 1991 U.S. pension funds invested about 3.4 percent of their holdings in emerging markets, but by 1995 the proportion had risen to roughly 13 percent. A straw in the wind: In late 1996, the state treasurers of California, Connecticut, and Ohio toured East Asia and pledged to invest more than $10 billion of their public pension fund money over the next two years.

Put another way, whether we realize it or not, we all will be buying a stake in the growth of the emerging markets. Our fortunes will literally rise and fall with theirs.

Business Strategies

The BEMs constitute the next big frontier for global business. American firms like General Electric, Boeing, Microsoft, Citibank, Ford, General Motors, Motorola, Coca-Cola and Procter & Gamble are all targeting these areas as the mainstay of their future growth. A quick look at some of the projections for market growth shows why business is so riveted on the possibilities.

Start with automobiles. Over the next few decades the purchase of cars in the United States, Western Europe, and Japan is projected to remain level at best. But as living standards rise all over Asia, Latin America, and Eastern Europe, the trend in those regions will be way up. In China, 600,000 cars were produced for the domestic market in 1995. Forecasters believe that by the year 2010, China will be making over 4 million vehicles for its people. Brazil produced 1.7 million cars in 1995; projections show production increasing to 2.2 million by 2005. The growth in the combined Brazilian and Argentine markets has led General Motors to plan for as much as $3 billion in new investments in these two countries between 1995 and 2000. Ford is planning nearly as much. Growth in car buying in India is increasing by 25 percent annually.

The big emerging markets are also supporting a good part of the commercial aircraft industry in America. Ten percent of all Boeing planes are now sold to China, supporting nearly 50,000 jobs a year in the United States, and competition to sell aircraft to India, Singapore, and other emerging markets is fierce. The energy industry shows a similar trend, with the International Energy Agency predicting that energy consumption in emerging markets will more than double by 2010, providing enormous opportunities for companies in energy development and management, as well as for engineering firms. In the telecommunications arena, China alone is expected to add 100 million phone lines in the next five years, equal to the entire number of phone lines already installed in the United States. It is expanding its power grid by the equivalent of one new Baby Bell per year. Indonesia is building a new infrastructure from scratch, requiring enormous investment and linkups with foreign firms.

Consumer goods industries also expect a bonanza. Over the past decade, Coca-Cola's soft drink sales in the United States have grown at the modest rate of 4.2 percent. Overseas, the prospects are dramatically different. The company projects that in China, India, and Indonesia sales should double every three years for the indefinite future.

Even U.S. defense contractors see lucrative markets in the BEMs. Taking Latin America as an example, Lockheed Martin Corporation is stepping up its activity in Argentina. Together with McDonnell Douglas, it is also competing for large aircraft orders in Brazil. During the Carter administration, a ban on U.S. military sales to most of Latin America was imposed because of extraordinary human rights abuses condoned by military dictatorships. Now, given the installation of democracies throughout the hemisphere since that time, the ban is likely to be lifted. In Asia, the United States and Russia are competing in countries like Thailand and Malaysia to sell sophisticated fighter planes and missiles.

Some of America's most powerful firms in the financial services industry are developing strategies based on assumptions that in a global economy the big emerging markets will have to be at the center of their attention. Morgan Stanley, one of the nation's most important investment banks, has focused heavily on setting up shop in China, India, and elsewhere. Between 1990 and 1995 its staff in Asia outside Japan increased from 90 to 540 people. Citibank has moved aggressively into consumer markets in Asia and Latin America, competing with local banks for individuals and small businesses, and aiming to be the preeminent lender to the rising middle classes from Bangkok to Buenos Aires.

———

It is easy to sound overexuberant about the commercial prospects for American firms in the BEMs. Without question, many of the superoptimistic projections for U.S. sales will never materialize. For more than a century, companies have made extravagant calculations about the lucrative potential of China or Brazil, only to be disappointed. This time, however, there is a good chance—the best in a century—that the commercial and financial possibilities in the Big Ten will be pivotal in terms of their importance to the U.S. economy and to American firms. Virtually all of the arrows are pointed in the right direction. Moreover, it is of crucial importance that the United States makes these economic links work, for our most vital national interests depend on it. With no major wars in sight, with all of the Big Ten moving toward more open markets, with our firms in strong, competitive positions—with all this, we have reason to be encouraged that the world economy and the Big Ten in particular can help us to build better and more secure lives. This is not to say that hurdles and risks do not exist, however. In fact, they are enormous.

3 The Risks of Economic Engagement

The increasing competitiveness of the big emerging markets will lead to bigger trade deficits and pressure on American workers.

The United States contends with a host of problems in the BEMs, including inadequate access to their markets, violation of intellectual property rights, corruption, and underhanded competition on the part of other industrial countries.

The risks of investing in the Big Ten are still substantial despite the enormous opportunities.

As my colleagues and I completed our study of Indonesia in the fall of 1993, we had also begun parallel examinations of China, India, and Brazil. The juxtaposition of these separate cases, all analyzed by different teams, made it clear that the economic opportunity for American firms and investors in these three countries was offset by a number of drawbacks. These included the growing competitiveness of the BEMs and the pressures their exports would put on our workforce. In addition, we would face a host of other problems—such as trade barriers that were too high, selective prohibitions against foreign investment, excessive red tape and regulation, violations of intellectual property rights, widespread corruption, and brutal competition from Europe and Japan. It became clear that while Americans needed the Big Ten's markets, we would face enormous obstacles to achieving our commercial goals.

Big Emerging Problems

TRADE DEFICITS

Many economists dismiss the idea that trade deficits are a major source of concern for the American economy. Although the size of the U.S. trade deficit remains large in absolute numbers—averaging over $150 billion per year between 1993 and 1995—as a proportion of our economy, it is small and declining. But the deficit is an easily watched number, and every month government reports show which countries account for the bulk of it. Politicians and many workers equate imports with a threat to established businesses, and the deficit therefore creates great anxiety in a society that is already worried about stagnant wages, corporate downsizing, and future job security.

In terms of absolute numbers (as opposed to percentage of GDP), the trade deficit itself has been resistant to reduction, except when our economy has been in recession. It doesn't seem to matter whether the dollar is weak or strong, or whether we are concluding a blizzard of market-opening trade agreements. In industry after industry, particularly in manufacturing, the growth of imports is strong, and is estimated to increase at an annual rate of 9 percent per year through the end of the century. Foreign automobiles, computer parts, toys, and construction equipment, among other goods, are all in growing demand in the United States.

Despite attempts by Ross Perot and Pat Buchanan to identify imports from low-wage countries as a major national problem, there has been no widespread political movement in America to do so. On the contrary, the Clinton administration was able to get congressional approval for a large number of trade agreements encompassing Canada, Mexico, Europe, Japan, and many other nations. In 1995, even as exports to Mexico slowed, the administration was citing polls showing that for the first time in memory, the majority of Americans thought trade was good for the economy. I sensed this feeling on my travels around the country during my time in the Clinton administration. To be sure, the sentiment wasn't usually, "Gosh, this trade expansion is a great thing for the United States." No, it was more a quiet resignation that in a global economy we had to play a certain game, and exporting and importing were part of it.

Nevertheless, some major changes are occurring in the structure of trade that could change popular attitudes. In particular, imports are likely to increase, especially from the BEMs, for the Big Ten are just now coming into their own with more products, more marketing savvy, and more experience in penetrating global markets. This coincides with a trend for more American firms to be forced to move some of their manufacturing plants abroad in search of lower costs, or in order to protect the foreign markets they already have. While most estimates show that the impact of emerging markets on the economies of the advanced industrial countries is relatively small today—3 to 5 percent of GDP—their significance to the American economy is bound to escalate significantly in the years ahead.

COLLISION WITH AMERICAN WORKERS

Experts from institutions as diverse as Harvard Business School, Kemper Financial Services in Chicago, and *The Economist* magazine are pointing to a freight train coming down the track—something on the order of one and a half billion productive people entering the mainstream global workforce in the next decade or so. Most of these people will be working for less than $10 a day, compared to most of their counterparts in the United States, Europe, and Japan, who will earn closer to $100 a day. Every case varies, of course, but the important point is the variance in wages. Boeing, for example, pays its machinists in China around $50 per month compared to $5,000 per month in Seattle. Elsewhere in China and in the other BEMs, the comparisons are even more stark. In the United States, the average hourly labor cost in manufacturing in 1995 was $17.20. In South Korea it was $7.40, in Taiwan $5.82, in Brazil

$4.28, in Poland $2.09, in Argentina $1.67, in Mexico $1.51, in China generally and India 25 cents. According to estimates by Professor Michael Jensen of the Harvard Business School, these Third World workers could produce at about 85 percent of the efficiency of Western workers, given the technology that is now being made available to them plus the Western management supervision and techniques being applied. These are rough estimates, but even if they are on the high side, it is clear that we are at the beginning of a massive shift in global production, and also, quite possibly, a long period of downward pressure on American wages as so much new production comes on stream. This freight train will hit as the impact of technology also transforms the American workforce, allowing existing firms to maintain or even increase their production by substituting machines for labor, and reducing their workforces by 20 to 30 percent. "What hangs in the balance," wrote Harvard Business School Professor Michael Porter, a leading authority on American competitiveness, "is our capacity to sustain wages that underpin our high standard of living."

Most economists would criticize this focus on the differences in wage rates. They would say that in the long run, compensation in low-wage countries will rise as workers there become more productive and as their living standards increase. They would also point to the benefits of low-cost goods to American consumers (who are, of course, also American workers) and the broader benefits of every country's producing what it does best (known in economics as the principle of comparative advantage). All of this is true in theory, but there will be severe disruptions along the way, and the "long term" could be far off in terms of the lives of men and women now in the workforce. American, European, and Japanese firms have been transferring the latest technology and management techniques to Asia as they build factories and pursue joint ventures, thereby increasing productivity and efficiency in the BEMs. But countries like South Korea and Taiwan, which have been increasing their productivity for a decade at least, pay hourly rates that still range from less than one-half to one-third of ours. This is not an argument for trade protection by any means, for it has been proven time and again that it is impossible to hold back the tides of commerce with trade barriers without weakening the economy as a whole. In fact, if it was difficult in past years, it is even more so today, given the unprecedented volume of trade, the need for U.S. firms to import many components in order to export finished products, and the cost to our economy of blocking lower-cost goods and services. But the surge of imports and the dislocation they can cause is reason to think hard about other policies to ensure that our workers have the tools to be as competitive as they can be, a subject discussed in chapter 7.

What will be the impact of the addition of 1.5 billion new, productive workers on the global scene? As one point of comparison, think of this: Japan, Taiwan, Hong Kong, South Korea, and Singapore—the dynamic five "Asian tigers" that have already sent major ripples through the world economy—have a combined population of fewer than 300 million people. Moreover, not only will there be a flood of new products from these billion-plus workers, but if current trends continue, America will be the prime destination, for ours is by far the most open economy. In the late 1980s we imported about 40 percent of all that East Asia had to sell to the world. Today that proportion is on the order of 25 percent, but climbing again. The share of Latin American products that we take is considerably higher. If you look at Europe's sky-high unemployment rates today, which hover around 10 to 12 percent, or at Japan's snail-like pace of deregulation and its prolonged economic slump, it appears that America will continue to be the destination of a disproportionate amount of the Big Ten's exports. Such a volume of goods reaching our shores could exert major downward pressure on U.S. wages. It could add to wage stagnation, to more layoffs, and to more difficulty in finding a new job at one's former wage level—all leading to serious social tensions in families and communities.

THE CASES OF CHINA, SINGAPORE, AND MEXICO

China is an illustration of things to come. In the late 1980s, the American trade deficit with China was negligible. Today China accounts for the second-largest portion of America's trade deficit, approaching $40 billion, and many analysts believe it will soon overtake Japan as the country with which we have the largest imbalance. China's exports to the United States have increased over thirtyfold since 1980, while our sales to China have "merely" quadrupled. In the past, moreover, China's exports to the United States were cheap textiles, shoes, and toys, but today an ever-larger percentage is composed of more sophisticated products such as computer peripherals and other electronic components, a trend that is sure to continue as more foreign investment pours into China. China's energetic labor force is becoming more highly trained at all levels, helped in large part by American firms. The quality of China's management will be upgraded as well, as American business schools—often in partnership with American firms—set up programs with major Chinese universities.

Singapore, a member of the broader ASEAN big emerging market, has a much higher annual per capita income than China—$20,000 versus $600—and the country's government and business leaders have decided that Singapore cannot compete with China's low-wage labor force. Instead they must move upscale into more technology-intensive products, where Singapore's highly skilled and educated workers would have a comparative advantage. The speed, scale, and, above all, the strategic deliberation with which the government and industry are moving are impressive. Three years ago, a consortium led by Texas Instruments opened Singapore's first modern chip-making facility. Now the government's goal is for this city-state of 2.9 million people to be one of the global centers for silicon chips. With tax incentives and other financial inducements, including offers to pay for specialized workforce training, Singapore is attracting new firms like Hitachi from Japan and Thomson Microelectronics, a French-

Italian company. The Singaporean government itself is an equity partner in several of the new ventures. Singaporean universities have started intensive programs to produce software engineers. Such is the competition our own chip makers face.

Mexico is another sensitive case. In the immediate aftermath of the NAFTA agreement, the United States sold much more to Mexico than vice versa; it appeared that we would run a large trade surplus for years to come. But when Mexico's financial crisis plunged the nation into deep recession in 1995, purchases from the United States declined precipitously. The Mexican peso was devalued against the dollar, and Mexican exports became much cheaper. Overnight America's trade surplus with Mexico turned into a trade deficit.

Seen from the standpoint of American workers whose companies compete with Mexican industry, the turnaround had high human costs. By the end of 1994, 17,320 workers had applied to Washington for assistance because they had lost their jobs as a result of imports from Mexico. A year later, the cumulative number had reached 52,000, and by May 1996 it stood at 72,136. For the people involved, these were traumatic events, to be sure, even though the U.S. economy was generating between 150,000 and 250,000 new jobs per month.

Some trends are especially sobering. Early in 1996, the Samsung Group, a South Korean conglomerate, opened an assembly line to produce TV sets in Tijuana. In so doing, Samsung moved one step closer to having as many Mexicans producing these sets for the U.S. market as there are Americans making the same products—some 30,000 workers. In Mexico the daily wage is about $9. In America, for this particular industry, it is about $50. The combination of advanced technology plus cheap labor seemed unbeatable, a trend that is sure to continue in this and other industries.

Competition in the United States from the big emerging markets is going to get much more intense in the years ahead. The measures that the BEMs have taken to build stronger economies, including privatizing their key industries, have yet to take full hold, but when they do we will be seeing countries that are vastly more competitive in the world arena. We will be faced not just with rising levels of imports produced with low-wage labor, but with products that reflect significant technological advances. World-class companies such as Acer in Taiwan, which produces computers and a wide range of electronics, or Samsung in South Korea, which is a large conglomerate with businesses ranging from aerospace to washing machines, have arisen in these regions, and they will challenge American firms not only in the United States but also in markets around the world. In addition, the local firms in many BEMs are being strengthened for the first time by mergers and foreign joint ventures that would not have been possible in the past, when economies were more tightly regulated. In Brazil, for example, more open markets and the taming of inflation have resulted in over 285 mergers and takeovers in the first nine months of 1996; half of these involved foreign companies which will bring capital, technology, and management to the table, as well as a global distribution system. American executives see the pattern. In a long-term assessment of U.S. competitiveness at the end of 1996, a quarter of the members of the bipartisan Council on Competitiveness—composed of the country's top corporate leadership—said that over the next decade the greatest source of competition for the United States would come from China, South Korea, India, Brazil, and Mexico.

BARGAINING AWAY TECHNOLOGY AND JOBS

As much anxiety as imports create, another trade-related phenomenon concerning big emerging markets can also be unsettling— firms that are moving abroad and making it easier for foreign workers to replace Americans, or to compete with them. A recent strike at Boeing tells the story.

Like other American firms, Boeing believes it must be in the China market in a big way. Moreover, if Boeing's chief rival, the

European Airbus consortium, were to acquire a leading market share in China, then Boeing's competitive position would be hurt all over the world, since Airbus would have the benefits not just of the China market but also of unprecedented economies of scale. As a condition of awarding contracts, however, Beijing is demanding that foreign firms transfer their latest technology to Chinese firms. From Beijing's standpoint this is the quid pro quo, because China wants to develop its own production capacity. It wants its workers able not just to understand the latest technology but to improve on it.

In 1995, 34,000 workers at Boeing went on strike over several issues relating to pay and security, including the transfer of technology to other markets There was no other way to do business in China, Boeing management said, and if the company wouldn't supply the technology, then Airbus surely would. Boeing's argument was that American workers would still retain the best jobs, and that the more prosperous Boeing became in the world market, the better off its employees would be. The alternative was a vastly diminished company, which would hurt workers much more than the technology transfer itself. In the end the Boeing strike was settled without Boeing giving way on the technology transfer question.

Boeing was not alone in its dilemma. Microsoft has entered into partnerships with over a dozen Chinese software houses. General Motors has agreed to help the Chinese design and build cars as the entry price to build its own $1 billion plant there. McDonnell Douglas, which is now merging with Boeing, has consented to co-produce planes in Shanghai. They all know that these activities will enhance China's ability to compete with us in the future. But the choice, as they see it, is to work with the Chinese, or not to do any business at all.

As American companies expand abroad, these issues will become increasingly common in labor negotiations. Governments all over Asia, Latin America, and Eastern Europe are making it more attractive for foreign companies to set up shop, building modern infrastructures, and educating their workforces. Singapore, as we have seen, has become a high-tech industrial city with a highly sophisticated labor force, and Malaysia is trying to create a multimedia corridor around its capital, with technology to attract the world's most sophisticated companies. Microsoft is rumored to be the first tenant.

But it isn't just that the investment climate is improving. The big emerging markets realize that they are in a strong bargaining position, often stronger even than the multinational companies, which until the 1990s seemed to have all the leverage. The reason for the shift in relative power is simple. If AT&T doesn't want to play by Chinese or Indian rules, if it doesn't want to transfer technology, train local workers, do research in the same market in which it is selling, commit to exporting a certain amount of its production and buying a certain amount of its supplies locally—all of which could take away jobs at home in the United States—then Japan's Nippon Telephone and Telegraph or France's Alcatel would be happy to do it. That's the game being played from Beijing to Brasilia.

How many American jobs will be lost is not clear, because there is ample evidence that when U.S. firms go abroad, they tend to buy many of their components from their parent companies in America, particularly those companies that require sophisticated technology. Foreign investment therefore stimulates American exports; in fact, some studies show that for every four dollars an America firm invests abroad in plant and equipment, its foreign operations then purchase $1 worth of goods and services from the United States. But the politics and psychology of a significant transfer of production from the United States to top big emerging markets are bound to be explosive, especially if the American economy slows down and unemployment rises.

These massive pressures make it inevitable that Americans will have to focus on the big emerging markets in a number of ways, all with the idea of mounting a relentless effort to keep foreign sales to the BEMs booming.

TRANSFER OF MILITARY TECHNOLOGY

Another kind of trade-related dilemma can arise when American companies sell technology for civilian uses that can also bolster a BEM's military capability. These so-called "dual use" technologies are often the subject of heated interagency debate in Washington, with the foreign policy agencies like the departments of State and Defense generally arguing to prohibit the sale, and the Department of Commerce, anxious to boost exports, looking for reasons to allow the transaction to go through. Commerce's position is not as purely mercantilist as it sounds. Often its argument rests on the fact that Washington, working with the BEM government in question, can satisfactorily monitor the use of the technology to ensure that it is not diverted to the military, or that the technology in question is readily available from many other commercial sources anyway. At the beginning of the Clinton administration, the list of technologies that it was prohibited to export was visibly reduced—particularly in the area of computers and telecommunications—reflecting the end of a Cold War mentality as well as the recognition that the United States didn't have a monopoly on much of the technology that was considered "dual use." In fact, President Clinton considered liberalization of export controls one of his major achievements in the trade area, and often touted it in public.

A recent case involving China revealed many of the delicate issues relating to dual-use technology. In 1994 McDonnell Douglas was trying to land a large contract to sell planes to China. The Chinese had requested that the plane manufacturer also supply certain machine tools to help them build aircraft in China. Since these same tools could be used to build missiles and other armaments, McDonnell Douglas obtained an export license from the Department of Commerce, in accordance with American law. The company won the aircraft deal, but it was subsequently discovered that the machine tools had been diverted to a Chinese military factory. In the fall of 1996 a federal grand jury was investigating what had happened. The McDonnell Douglas deal is cause for extra caution about how Washington balances its commercial and national security goals in the Big Ten and how and when it issues export licenses. The capability to monitor what happens after the sale is, of course, crucial, and no administration should be blinded by the fact that the commercial stakes in the BEMs can seem overwhelming. It will be increasingly important to take the possibility of military diversion of technology into account as we balance our economic and our national security concerns, and as these overlap in the Big Ten, as they so often will.

Closed and Distorted Markets

One issue on which America will have to continue to campaign aggressively is the removal of barriers to our exports and our investments. With very few exceptions, the BEMs, while moving toward more openness, place serious obstacles in the way of sales of American products and services, and of the establishment of foreign commercial facilities within their borders. The problems run the gamut—from high tariffs on the import of cars in Brazil to regulations that shut out foreign insurance companies in India.

THE CASE OF SOUTH KOREA

A particularly egregious example of a closed market is South Korea. It is important, because the United States is blocked from a potentially highly lucrative market even as Korean firms have free run of ours. Last year, for example, Korean per capita income reached $10,000, giving the country more purchasing power than virtually any other BEM and making it enormously attractive for such American companies as Whirlpool, Estée Lauder, Levi Strauss, and McDonald's. Korea is also important because of the military links between Seoul and Washington, which could be undermined by South Korea's barriers to American exports and investment.

A strong antiforeign bias has characterized South Korea's economic dealings for several decades. Tariffs are high—25 percent on average in 1995—and the government systematically discriminates against foreign companies in awarding construction and infrastructure projects. The regulatory environment is characterized by laws and regulations framed so generally that bureaucratic officials easily use them to harass foreign firms. The anti-import sentiment of the government is often revealed in long delays in customs clearance, and even in threats to conduct tax audits of South Korean companies that import. Major South Korean conglomerates are immune from antitrust policies, and are able to dominate the economy by sheer size. It is no wonder that in 1993, at a time when foreign investment around the world was mushrooming, thirty-one American firms either reduced their investments in South Korea or left altogether.

Nevertheless, the battle for the South Korean market, potentially one of the most lucrative of the BEMs, goes on. But as we bring pressure to bear on the Big Ten, we must be prepared for resistance. In principle, all the BEMs are signing on to the benefits of open markets, but, in practice, most of them want more time to make the transition from a government-controlled economy to a free market, and most feel that the United States is demanding that they move too fast.

INTELLECTUAL PROPERTY RIGHTS

One of the most difficult problems the United States faces in big emerging markets is the absence of fundamental legal foundations for free markets. As legal scholars like to say, there is an absence of "the rule of law." In other words, the BEMs do not have adequate laws and enforcement capabilities to run open economies where laws govern, where such laws are known to all, and where they are enforced. Instead, personal relationships are the key element in doing business. A classic case of deficiencies in the rule of law relates to the protection of "intellectual property rights"—copyrights, patents, trademarks.

Protecting the I.P.R. of American firms is one of Washington's highest trade priorities. Because so much of what we export these days—software, films, television shows—contains the fruits of research and inventions for which we want to be paid, products containing intellectual property have become the leading edge of American competitiveness. It is one of our answers to how we plan to compete with low-paid foreign workers, who wouldn't ordinarily have the ability to generate these same goods or services. It is no surprise that Washington and American firms are livid when companies in other countries steal our intellectual property for their own use or for resale. On a global basis, the magnitude of this problem is enormous. U.S. businesses in the software industry lose $15 billion a year to counterfeiters, and the U.S. movie industry loses about $2 billion. The problem has reached epidemic proportions in Asia, where movies and compact disks are illegally fabricated and sold on the streets. Illegal copies of *The Lion King*, for example, were seen all over Asia even before the movie was released in U.S. theaters. American firms have alleged that violations of I.P.R. in China alone have cost them over $2 billion in lost sales in 1995. American pharmaceutical companies have also had trouble in Latin America, particularly in Argentina, where historically there has been no patent protection at all.

At their roots, these conflicts over I.P.R. have deep historical and cultural dimensions. Americans have developed laws and institutions that reward a person's achievement—not surprising in a culture that places individual freedom at the very top of its value system. But consider the system in China, where there is no such tradition. There the art of copying has been held up for centuries as a rare talent, and the collective community has always taken precedence over the individual. In fact, American problems with China over I.P.R. are not new. The first intellectual property agreement with Beijing was signed in 1905, and yet in 1923 the bilingual version of Webster's Dictionary was on sale in China well before Webster intended to market it there.

Although China represents one of the most serious large-scale problems, it is not the only country in Washington's sights on this issue. In fact, in April 1996 the U.S. trade representative pointed to a large number of countries that were violating American I.P.R. laws. These included several European countries and Japan, but also many big emerging markets: Argentina, Turkey, India, South Korea, as well as two ASEAN members, the Philippines and Thailand. Washington has used trade sanctions, or the threat of them, to pressure many of these countries to respect I.P.R. and has encouraged joint ventures between U.S. firms and their foreign counterparts to enhance control over American products and services. The administration has also provided technical assistance to customs authorities and government officials charged with developing laws to protect intellectual property and to officials charged with enforcing them.

But it is slow going. In most cases, the issue isn't the law itself but effective enforcement of the law—which requires an independent judiciary system, an honest police force, an honest government. In addition, with the technology of pirating advancing so quickly, the problem may get much worse before it gets better. New presses to copy compact disks that are smaller and more efficient are being manufactured. Digital technology will soon increase the compression and quality of movies so that they can fit onto one disk, making counterfeiting far easier than ever before. The financial incentives for stealing are overwhelming, and the market among these large populations in the Big Ten is highly lucrative.

CORRUPTION

Another example of where the rule of law is lacking is the widespread corruption that exists in virtually all the big emerging markets, with Hong Kong and Singapore being the most notable exceptions. It is often difficult to do business in any of these countries without bribing someone. And with the flood of new business, the influx of foreign firms, and the competition to enter these new markets, corruption may be increasing. Indeed, chaos reins in the business climates of most of the Big Ten. It's every person for himself, as the desire to get rich quick is overwhelming. In such situations, payoffs are a part of winning contracts, getting a project completed, or obtaining vital supplies through customs. With government-based economies giving sway to market-oriented systems, the old rules are breaking down, but no adequate regulations exist to take their place. The police are overstretched, and often corrupt themselves. The courts are clogged and rarely prosecute, except in a few high-profile instances.

Corruption is as old as civilization, and no country is without it. In the Big Ten, however, the issue is its pervasive nature. Consider the first eight months of 1996 alone. The Mexican government had a major money-laundering and corruption scandal on its hands with the investigation of Raul Salinas, brother to the former president, Carlos Salinas, who on his $190,000 salary managed to amass a fortune estimated at about $200 million. In August of 1996, moreover, the Mexican government dismissed more than 700 of the 4,400 officers in the federal judicial police to root out "all the irregularities, all the anarchy," according to Attorney General Antonio Lozano Gracia. In India, prosecutors went after the former prime minister, P. V. Narashima Rao, three of his ministers, and many other top leaders for taking bribes. In Turkey, former prime minister Tansu Cillar was under investigation for allegedly profiting handsomely from selloffs of state companies. In Indonesia, the relatives of President Suharto were getting exceedingly wealthy through special tax breaks for all of their businesses. In Argentina, ninety-five officials linked to the government of President Carlos Menem faced corruption investigations.

Complicating matters is the fact that American firms are the only companies subjected to tough criminal penalties for bribery, because only the United States has domestic legislation—the Foreign Corrupt Practices Act—that focuses so intensely on illegal payments overseas. By contrast, German and Canadian firms have historically been allowed to take tax write-offs for "the costs of doing business." French and Japanese firms also routinely provide payoffs of one kind or another without penalties at home. The Department of Commerce estimates that because of bribery by foreign firms, since mid-1994 U.S. firms have lost contracts valued at approximately $11 billion—and these are only the high-profile cases that American firms report.

CUTTHROAT FOREIGN COMPETITION

Bribery is just a part of a larger problem—the ferocious and often underhanded competition that takes place among American, European, and Japanese firms to win the enormous contracts that are being awarded in big emerging markets. This competition is being waged on several levels. For example, Tokyo, Paris, and Washington vie with one another to provide low-cost financing and insurance for their firms trying to win projects in the emerging markets. Global trade rules say that such help is acceptable, because it supports jobs in the home country of the winning companies. What is not acceptable under our trade agreements, but what happens nevertheless, is that these trade loans are mixed with foreign aid. The double inducement—low-cost loans for a company and free money to the government awarding the contract—is hard to beat.

Again, in this game American firms operate at a big disadvantage. Washington's foreign aid is declining, and it is, in any event, earmarked for social projects like clean water or housing. In addition, Congress would strenuously oppose using taxpayers' money to subsidize American exports. Europe and Japan have no such problems. Their aid programs remain large, and, for the most part, their decision making is shrouded in complicated and secretive bureaucratic procedures, ensuring that the public has no clear understanding of how the money is being used.

Another kind of competition has to do with the extent to which our competitors' foreign policy has been geared toward commercial goals. In recent years, the president of France, the chancellor of Germany, and the prime ministers of England, Canada, and Japan have all made multiple commercial missions to help sell their countries' products and to smooth the way for their firms' activities in the big emerging markets. They carry with them large loan offers, foreign aid, and even promises of certain changes in foreign policy. From the beginning, the Clinton administration has felt it has little choice but to make sure that American firms receive significant support in order not to lose out to their rivals. The high-profile trade missions of Secretary Brown and the personal intervention of President Clinton and other cabinet members in certain important deals with countries like Brazil or Saudi Arabia have given Washington a new image. It is one of an administration that assigns a very high priority to its commercial goals in big emerging markets, ranking them alongside other top foreign policy goals such as maintaining good relationships abroad or even preserving strong military ties.

Still, it is questionable how long this American zeal will last, for it is certainly not as rooted in the American culture as it is in that of our commercial rivals, who have put business goals at the center of their foreign policy for many decades. Already American policies are being eroded as a result of political infighting in Washington. Some in Congress want to use the 1996 revelations of illegal foreign campaign contributions to demolish the institutions that conduct our global commercial policies, such as the Commerce Department, the Export-Import Bank, and the Overseas Private Investment Corporation. To the extent that they are linking two different issues—the need for campaign reform and the aggressive pursuit of our commercial and foreign policy interests—they are deviously and ingenuously following a purely political agenda of weakening the administration, whatever the consequences for our vital global interests. Another group, which no doubt contains much overlap with the first, is alleging that government-supported export promotion constitutes "corporate welfare." I know from first-hand experience with Congress that most of the critics of export promotion do not have even a rudimentary understanding of the programs. They have a visceral sense that money is being wasted, but not much more. Their concerns must be addressed, of course, but surely our vital national interests will suffer if we cannot sort out the issues of campaign finance, organizational efficiency and fiscal discipline without crippling our ability to play according to the rules of a fiercely competitive global marketplace.

This much is for sure: The stakes in the big emerging markets are too large to assume that our European and Japanese competitors will not accelerate *their* efforts—by whatever measures necessary—to achieve greater market share in these countries.

Brutal as the competition has been, it is only in its early stages. The advanced industrialized countries see more clearly than ever how important the BEMs are to their economic growth, the competitiveness of their firms, and their job base. With slow growth in all the main industrial countries, high unemployment in Europe, stagnation in Japan, and with all major governments cutting back on spending, exports will become a crucial source of stimulus and the quest for foreign markets is sure to intensify.

THE RISKY ECONOMIC LANDSCAPE

As American citizens focus on investing in the Big Ten and other emerging markets, caution is in order. Emerging markets are risky, even as they are an increasingly important component of any major portfolio. As we will see in the forthcoming chapters, the politics of economic reform is tension-ridden and uncertain, and the prospect for serious instability is all too real. In addition, the computer technology that makes it so easy for Fidelity Investments or Lehman Brothers to move money into emerging markets can act in reverse; at the slightest hint of trouble, billions of dollars can be instantly withdrawn, deflating the very markets they held up.

The financial returns on investments in emerging markets tend to be highly volatile as well, for emerging market securities tend to fluctuate much more violently than, say, the S&P 500. To take one example, in 1993 an index of emerging market stocks would have returned 67.5 percent, compared to 10 percent for the S&P 500 index. In 1995, largely because of the global impact of the Mexican peso crisis, a key emerging market index (maintained by the World Bank), was down 12.3 percent while the S&P was up 37.4 percent. This said, even amidst volatility, emerging market stocks have done well over the January 1991–September 1996 period. A Morgan Stanley index, for example, achieved an annual rate of 18.80 percent, compared to 15.92 percent for the S&P. The upshot is that over time, it is a good bet that a diversified portfolio of U.S. and foreign stocks—including some from emerging markets—will outperform a strictly U.S. portfolio. However, unless one has a very high tolerance for risk, heavy investing in these countries is best left to institutional investors who can weather the violent fluctuations.

Moreover, investors should not be fooled into believing that the stock markets in the Big Ten are regulated in a way that inspires confidence. Although standards are improving, nowhere are they up to U.S. practices. The rules protecting shareholders are spotty, as voting, enforcement of the laws, responsibilities and liabilities of corporate boards of directors all vary considerably. Insider trading can be rampant, and markets can be dominated by just a few companies, many of which are still owned by families whose interests diverge from those of outside shareholders.

There are other reasons for caution. A rise in interest rates in the major Western markets would surely induce capital flows out of big emerging markets to New York or London, where the funds would be earning more. This is a particular concern for the Latin American BEMs—Mexico, Brazil, and Argentina—because they all have very low domestic savings rates and are consequently heavily dependent on the inflows of foreign capital. An upsurge in protectionism in the West could damage the BEMs' economic prospects as well, for if they found themselves importing too much and selling too little abroad, their trade deficits would grow too large, and they could then be forced to devalue their currencies to make their exports cheaper and more competitive. Devaluations, however, make foreign investors nervous because the value of their investments, measured in their home currencies, is also reduced. That's what started the panic in Mexico in the winter of 1994–95: The devaluation of the peso meant that when Americans exchanged their investments in Mexico for dollars, they would receive far fewer greenbacks than they expected. Not knowing how and when this downward spiral would end, foreign investors demanded to get out of their Mexican investments right away.

In Asia, especially, investors run the risk that there will be an oversupply in certain products as all countries vie with one another in the same industries. The classic case is electronics—personal computers, circuit boards, desk drives, memory chips—but overcapacity is also a potential problem in automobiles and chemical processing. Today Singapore, Taiwan, and South Korea are the acknowledged leaders in these businesses, but China, Indonesia, and Vietnam could enter the fray as well, with lightning speed. For countries so heavily dependent on exports for their economic growth, a glut in an industry would drive prices down, reduce revenues from foreign sales, and potentially cause a new bout of protectionism in the United States and Europe as imports surge into our markets.

The Achilles heel of the entire system, however, is the possibility that the growth of world trade will slow dramatically. Some deceleration was already evident in 1996 compared to 1995, but it is too early to call this a trend. If the trade balances of the Big Ten deteriorate significantly—if the imports of these countries exceed exports by too large a margin—the BEMs may be forced to slow down their economies with higher interest rates. This would reduce their imports, putting pressure on Western export-dependent economies. Or, if instead of raising interest rates the Big Ten decide to erect new protectionist barriers to slow their imports, there could be retaliation from abroad.

Another scenario for a slowdown in trade is a recession in the United States combined with growing frustration in America with stagnant wages and layoffs, and a charismatic populist leader who fires up disaffected workers and the Congress, leading to a swing toward protectionism. A similar series of events could be even more likely in Europe, where over one in ten workers is now unemployed. Any protectionism in the West would be a hammer blow to big emerging markets because of their heavy dependence on exports.

It is entirely reasonable to expect that there will be more financial crises, too. The essence of big emerging markets is that they are making the transition from one stage of development to another. This is a dangerous time for them and us, because it means that everything is in flux—especially regulations and supervision. There is an air of chaos, with sporadic influxes of large sums of money, inadequate information and disclosure, and speculative drives. Experienced financial officials are in short supply and lack sufficiently skilled staff. The Mexican financial crisis of 1995 took the entire world by surprise and shook the foundation of the international financial system. In November of 1994, President Clinton was holding up Mexico as the "poster boy" of economic reform. One month later the peso collapsed. It would be naïve to say that this couldn't happen to another big emerging market.

———

For America, the rewards of economic engagement with the Big Ten can be enormous. But the obstacles to achieving our economic goals are daunting. It is essential that we develop approaches to the BEMs that navigate this winding road. It is crucial that we understand the stakes and take a long-term perspective. In the short run, there will be great frustrations as we interact with societies in the middle of difficult and chaotic transitions. But over time, we have no choice but to engage the Big Ten in order to safeguard our interests.

4 Beyond Economics: Political Power and Political Instability

Trade and finance are only one dimension of America's necessary engagement with the Big Ten. Their political power is another.

We must pay attention to the potential political and economic instability of the BEMs, too, because their own problems could easily become ours.

Thus, both their strength and their weakness constitute the political significance of the big emerging markets.

IN THE EARLY STAGES of the Clinton administration's strategy toward the Big Ten, virtually all the effort went into export promotion. Commerce Secretary Brown's presentations within the administration and his public appearances, as well as mine, focused on commercial opportunities and the obstacles to achieving them. It wasn't that we didn't understand that the big emerging markets were becoming powerful political players. We knew that economic drives had enormous political and strategic implications, and we were aware of the increasing decibel level of BEMs in international negotiations around the world on every major issue from foreign investment to human rights. But the fact is that the structure of the U.S. executive branch often makes it very difficult to link economics and foreign policy, for decision making is heavily compartmentalized into boxes, each of which is governed by the traditional mind-set of a different group of policy makers. For the State Department, the top priorities were NATO, Russia, the Middle East peace negotiations, Bosnia, Somalia, Haiti. Significant attention was also paid to nuclear weapons in North Korea and the United States–Japan Security Treaty. China and Mexico received a good deal of attention, too. But at no time was there an overall review of our changing interests in the BEMs, or of our need for a longer-term, comprehensive strategy toward these nations. As a result, the government had the beginnings of an international commercial policy, but not a new foreign policy. The second Clinton administration could do much better, and thereby set the stage for changes in our most fundamental international strategies as we head into a new century.

———

The movement of economic power to the big emerging markets, with all its positive and disturbing dimensions, gives the Big Ten a degree of political leverage on the global scene that would have been unimaginable just a few years ago. It would be a mistake, however, to think of BEMs *solely* as economic or trading entities, for they all represent strong political forces in their own right and occupy pivotal positions in international trade and finance, in international organizations, and on issues as diverse as nuclear nonproliferation and human rights.

The conventional wisdom is that the best way to ensure that these nations act peacefully and cooperatively is to encourage them to participate fully in the international institutions that have been built up over the past fifty years—the web of global organizations and arrangements stretching from agreements not to test nuclear weapons to a host of agencies such as the World Trade Organization. If certain big emerging markets are already part of this Western global framework, so the argument goes, then we should work more closely with them in order to deepen cooperation. If they are not actively participating members—or, as in the case of China and the World Trade Organization, not members at all—then they should be drawn into the web. In the spring of 1996 an article in *Foreign Affairs* put it succinctly: "The problems the liberal democratic order confronts are mostly problems of success, foremost among them the need to integrate the newly developing and post-Communist countries. Here one sees most clearly that the post–Cold War order is really a continuation and extension of the Western order forged during and after World War II."

It won't be so easy. International life has become much more complicated with the demise of the two rival camps led by Washington and Moscow. So long as that contest existed, getting new members into one club or the other was helped by political pressure to huddle under the security umbrella of one of the superpowers. But with that need removed, the big emerging markets feel much less obligated to adopt anyone's rules unless they deem it to be in their own interests to do so.

To be sure, often they will see it that way. For example, the pressure to adhere to free-market economic policies is compelling for Poland, not because Uncle Sam says to do it, but because the global financial markets, representing investors everywhere, penalize countries whose policies go astray. Likewise, the people of Argentina decided to downsize their military because they felt it was important for fiscal reasons, and to purge the militarism that had once dominated the country.

It's not that the big emerging markets are hostile to what America wants; it's that they are likely in the future to march to their own drummers whenever possible. They will be more self-confident and more assertive. As they advance economically, they are likely to take more satisfaction in their own accomplishments, and this could well translate into more pride in their own national heritage and into a stronger nationalism. They will be—indeed, they already are—much freer to be themselves.

The rise of the big emerging markets is so recent that it is impossible to predict where their newfound sense of liberation will lead them. But unless the behavior of nations and the people who run them have changed forever, power has a way of growing until it meets with some resistance. It would be dangerous to assume that just because the BEMs are currently preoccupied with economic development and see their economic progress as the key to everything else, they have permanently forgone the militarism that has

characterized political entities—cities, city-states, empires, and nations—throughout history.

Geopolitical Players

It is certain that the big emerging markets will play a key role in
areas of major geopolitical tensions. China's political and military
power is already altering the shape of security policy in Asia. Its army
is growing and it has shown a willingness to confront neighbors on a
wide range of border disputes. It has lobbed missiles perilously close
to Taiwan. It has shown thinly veiled disdain for Japan, and harbors
suspicions left over from World War II that Tokyo will again cast a
military shadow over Asia. Beijing has been critical of the United
States–Japan Security Treaty on the grounds that it could be interpreted as being aimed against China. In the future, as China's power
grows, Beijing's apprehensions could well shape the relationship between Washington and Tokyo as each tries to curry favor with Beijing
or avoid its wrath.

Elsewhere, the historic hostility between India and Pakistan remains a tinderbox, given that both nations have nuclear capabilities.
The emotions, the population pressures, the historical enmities all
make this standoff one of the most dangerous anywhere. The problems between South and North Korea are a long way from being
solved, and there remains the possibility of a major war on that penin-
sula, one that could drag in the United States, Japan, and China.

Turkey, too, has great geopolitical importance. As a land bridge
between Europe and Asia, it is a potential bulwark against the
spread of Islamic fundamentalism from the Persian Gulf. Being so
close to the newly independent countries on the southern flank of
the former Soviet Union, it is also a strategic gateway to several
heretofore closed societies with substantial reserves of oil and other
minerals. It is in this region that enormous pipelines for oil and gas
are being installed, and huge investments contemplated—all but

insuring an explosive mix of national politics and global business forces—with Ankara in a pivotal geographical position.

NEW ECONOMIC EMPIRES

Another way that BEMs could exercise power is through the political influence of new trade arrangements. It was not so long ago that Washington touted the extension of NAFTA all the way to Argentina and Chile. This would have created a trade region very much under U.S. influence because the enlarged NAFTA would have been based on rules approved by the United States, extending American-style labor standards and environmental protection from Point Barrow to Cape Horn, and providing American firms with significant advantages. But two developments occurred to prevent NAFTA's enlargement. First, the U.S. Congress refused to give the Clinton administration legal authority to incorporate Chile as a fourth member. After the heated debate over free trade with Mexico, and particularly after the collapse of the Mexican economy and the dramatic slowdown of American exports there, there was simply too much controversy in Washington about admitting a new member to the NAFTA club. Meanwhile, Brazil was busy developing the Mercosur regional trading bloc and Chile, tired of waiting for the Americans to move, joined up with its neighbors.

Several years ago, such developments might have been greeted with a yawn by global strategists. Some old Cold War warriors who still count soldiers and missiles continue to be unimpressed. But they miss the picture of how power is changing. In the case of Mercosur, Brazil will have great influence over the pace of trade liberalization in a vast area of the world—several huge markets encompassing nearly 250 million people, with a combined GDP of over $1 trillion, with sizable middle classes and enormous purchasing power and infrastructure needs. Mercosur borders on both the Atlantic and Pacific oceans, and it has already begun to seek trade agreements with Europe and with Asia. It will have a much stronger voice over new trade rules relating to foreign investment, workers' rights, and environmental protection. When it comes time for America to negotiate with Brazil or with any individual member of the Mercosur group, it may soon have to face the group as a whole because their economies will have become intertwined. Mercosur as a bloc will have much more bargaining clout than any one of its individual members. This will not be a happy event for us, not after having called the shots in the Western Hemisphere for so long.

The way of thinking about global politics and economics in the southern cone of our hemisphere is much different from how it appears from key parts of the United States. Washington still thinks of itself as the political capital of the hemisphere. But in my frequent trips to Argentina and Brazil for the Clinton administration, I saw a much different picture. Washington's views are heavily discounted. American foreign policy is seen as consisting of short-term reflexes to domestic political problems, with no overall grand design, and little relevance to the big emerging markets in the southern portion of our hemisphere. American politics is of decreasing interest to countries with more self-confidence and overwhelming domestic political preoccupations of their own. This situation is radically different from the intensive focus on everything that happened in Washington during the Cold War days.

These attitudes were characteristic of the most prominent and powerful businessmen in the region, the people who invest in bricks and mortar, who market products and services, and who write paychecks. They were not preoccupied with the American market or NAFTA. Their main priority is to expand trade and investment much closer to home. The Argentines see Brazil as the market of the future. The Brazilians see their neighboring countries as having great potential. It was clear to me that the growth of this economic empire thousands of miles south of Miami is based not on some politician's dream but on the visions and drives of businesses on the ground. It could become a formidable entity.

Mercosur is but one example of the trend toward emerging

market "empires." Another is "the Chinese Economic Area"—the People's Republic of China, Hong Kong, and Taiwan. Taken together, this big emerging market will combine a powerful military complex with one of the world's largest potential markets, and with perhaps the largest hoard of foreign exchange reserves anywhere. Its 1 billion plus population, with increasing levels of education, contains incalculable human energy. If this market becomes tightly integrated, as is likely to happen because of expanding trade and investment, it will change the economic and political face of the world.

ASEAN is another powerful pole in Asia. If economic growth and intraregional trade continue at even half the breakneck pace of past years—and there's every chance that this will happen—then within five years America will be selling more goods to ASEAN than to China and India combined. Here, too, is a region where economic power will translate into political power, for ASEAN is developing a group outlook when it comes to military matters. It will soon be impossible for U.S. troops to operate flexibly in Southeast Asia, as we have done in the past, without getting at least the acquiescence of the ASEAN group.

Influence in International Organizations

The big emerging markets will exercise significant political power within international organizations. In the last months of 1994, I had the opportunity to participate in the final round of the global trade negotiations known as the "Uruguay Round" in Geneva. It was an occasion not just to spend all-nighters wrestling with technical trading rules, but also to observe how various countries behaved. One would have expected that the Europeans would wield a lot of clout, and they did. But what really surprised me was the skill and energy of negotiators from Hong Kong, Singapore, other ASEAN nations like Thailand, as well as Brazil and India. These men and women had a superb grip on the trading rules and how to negotiate them. They also had a strategic concept of how they wanted to shape the new World Trade Organization—which was being established by these very negotiations—and what they wanted the new body to accomplish. (This was in great contrast to the main industrial powers, who had barely thought through what the new organization would do and what its longer-term implications were.) Sitting there in Geneva, I had no doubt that the voices and influence of the big emerging markets in the evolution of how international trade would be managed in the future would grow exponentially. It's happening already. ASEAN, for example, has its own very strong ideas when it comes to human rights and trade, or labor standards and trade—ideas that run contrary to Washington's official position. And ASEAN is making them known very effectively in the World Trade Organization, exercising a de facto veto on how much pressure the United States and Europe can exert on the institution.

It is not just in trade organizations where these countries will wield power and influence. In the summer of 1996, India defied the world on the issue of arms control. Standing against the United States, Russia, England, France, and China, New Delhi refused to sign a comprehensive nuclear test ban treaty. Why? It felt insecure swearing off the nuclear option in the face of distrust of its three nuclear neighbors—Pakistan, China, Russia. Such insecurity is understandable enough, but the significance of the event was India's willingness to stand alone against so much outside pressure. An Indian newspaper captured the mood: "In blocking the passage of [the Comprehensive Test Ban Treaty] India has shown a rare diplomatic self-assurance . . . For too long in the recent past, the very murmur of disapproval from the great powers on a particular issue often stopped Indian policy in its tracks. In the last few years, India was ready to catch a cold even before Washington sneezed." As a result of India's objections, gaining passage of the treaty in the United Nations became much more difficult.

Power of Monetary Reserves

Over the last decade, the big emerging markets, particularly in Asia, have been amassing significant currency reserves which will give them not only the financial power to expand their investments and purchasing power, but also a larger voice in how the monetary system will be governed. The shift of economic power to Asia has been gradual but steady. Today, for example, America's reserves (excluding gold) are on the order of $75 billion. Germany has about $85 billion, and Japan has about $185 billion. But the total reserves of China, Taiwan, Hong Kong, South Korea, and the ASEAN countries amount to more than $340 billion. The significance of these numbers is that the Asian BEMs will be in a strong position to withstand economic shocks, and they will have more money than other nations to finance their national development. They will also be able to use their reserves to buy and sell other currencies in order to make sure their own currency stays in a range that maintains highly competitive prices for the products they sell. In short, in an era where economic strength equates to raw political power and influence, they will be heavily armed.

Scramble for Energy

In Asia, the scramble for global energy sources presents another geopolitical flashpoint for the Big Ten. Demand for energy is growing more rapidly in the region than anywhere else. Until 1993, for example, China was a net oil exporter. In 1996 it was due to import about 600,000 barrels a day. Within fifteen years imports are projected to grow by over 400 percent to some 2.7 million barrels per day. ASEAN's rapid industrialization will require enormous increments of energy. If South and North Korea unite, creating a major industrial powerhouse, large new energy requirements will result as well.

The OPEC countries, particularly those of the Middle East, are expected to provide the overwhelming amount of the BEMs' oil needs. Potentially, this puts the Asian big emerging markets on a political collision course with the United States when it comes to isolating countries like Iran and Iraq, for the Asian BEMs are not likely to antagonize their vital suppliers. A lot of oil could also come from regions of the former Soviet Union such as Kazakhstan, raising the prospect of big-power oil and pipeline politics involving the entire span of countries from Turkey to Japan. Farfetched as it might sound today, it is not out of the question that China, Japan, and South Korea would come to military blows over oil, causing the United States to enter the confrontation in order to stop a war in Asia that affects our economic interests.

The Clash of Politics and Economics

The political challenges the United States faces extend beyond the broad geopolitical chessboard. Equally important will be our frustrations with the interaction of political and economic changes, and the detours that many big emerging markets will take from democracy and free markets in the next several years.

During the Cold War, Americans pressed Third World nations to become democracies. We genuinely felt more comfortable with nations that were like us—nations that elected their leaders, valued open expression, and protected human rights. We believed that democracies would spawn free-market economies, which would give us more business opportunities and also more trade and economic links to influence these countries. And, as our post–World War II foreign policy demonstrated, from the early days with Germany and Japan, to later events in Vietnam, Nicaragua, and elsewhere, our interest in shoring up democracies was intensified by the fear that if countries were not allied with us, they would be strong-armed into joining the enemy camp.

Today our interest in democracy has strong elements of idealism, but it has little to do with fears of Communist infiltration. We still think that democratic politics makes for good economics, but events may soon compel us to become much more sober about this linkage. Indeed, one of the biggest problems that America will face is the coming political chaos in the big emerging markets as their fragile democracies confront the requirements for hard economic choices.

Over the long term, democracy and free markets do go hand in hand. They both facilitate free choice and free expression. They both give individuals a chance to participate in the affairs of their communities and countries, and they provide some balance between equality of opportunity and recognition of merit and hard work. In today's entrepreneurial world economy, moreover, there is more need than ever to allow individual initiative to flourish. And the impact of the communications revolution, with easy access to phones, faxes, and the Internet, will so empower individuals that no tightly controlled, centralized, undemocratic government stands a chance of being successful for too long.

It's easy to agree on the goal of more firmly rooted democracy and sensibly regulated free markets. The trouble comes when a country is in the process of transition from a system with no democratic tradition to a full-fledged democracy, or when it is in the process of moving from a closed economy to an open one—and particularly when it is doing both at the same time. These transitions are a recipe for political instability, political paralysis, inconsistent economic policies, and economic backtracking.

Immature democracies do not constitute effective government, because they lack a solid foundation for representing the people. In South Korea, China, Indonesia, Mexico, or Brazil, for example, personal relationships, not the rule of law, tend to dominate how things get done. These countries do not have the right institutions in place, such as an impartial and independent judicial system, or regulations relating to stock markets or to excessive concentration of corporate power. They do not have a system of checks and balances to protect the nation's longer-term interests from more immediate public passions. They do not have a way to channel popular frustrations so that their citizens can feel they are being heard and that something will be done to deal with their problems—a critical safety valve in any society, but particularly in those undergoing tumultuous transitions. They do not have the right kind of people in government, for the civil service is often poorly trained and riddled with corruption.

Infant democracies under pressure usually appeal to tribal, ethnic, and religious groups in their society. As centralized totalitarian controls are dismantled, there is widespread room for criminal and corrupt elements to roam free. Whole systems are breaking down, and new ones are not being established fast enough to impose order. Meanwhile economic progress continues, but in an extremely Darwinian environment in which inequalities of living standards widen, creating even more political problems. The historian Donald Kagan once set out the three conditions on which democratic governance rests—a set of good institutions, a body of citizens who understand what democracy is all about, and a high quality of leadership at critical moments. For most of the BEMs it will be a long time before all of those qualities are in place.

The interaction of democratic evolution and economic liberalization is truly explosive. The two sets of forces, combined with the growing pressures of trade and technology, represent a frontal threat to a society's ability to govern itself. Public and private agendas are too overloaded to be implemented smoothly, and expectations that simply cannot be met are aroused. Citizens think they will be more equal because democracy is supposed to give them a voice equal to that of every other citizen. But capitalism works in a different way: It tends to widen the inequalities, especially when governments' resources are strained. Indeed, some of the great global fortunes are being built right now in emerging markets under circumstances that mirror the free-wheeling, chaotic, and near-lawless society that characterized America in the robber baron days. In our country, that environment eventually led to a major political backlash, including a wave of populist pressures and extensive regulation, but it took several decades. Today, given the ease of communication, the potential for a mass overreaction to perceived inequities in the BEMs is even greater than it was for us.

THE STAKES FOR AMERICA

All of the big emerging markets have varying degrees of these interlocking political and economic problems. How they are resolved is of crucial interest to the United States. Strong democracies will be much less likely to precipitate a war. They will be more reliable partners in diplomacy and trade, and they will be much more protective of human rights.

Because of our growing business and financial interests, Americans have a pressing interest in the continuation of economic reforms. Without progress on sound monetary and budget problems, which hold down inflation and keep foreign money coming in, and without continued reduction of trade barriers and deregulation within the big emerging markets, American sales would slow. Consequently, the pace of our economic growth, our companies' profits, and our jobs would be impaired.

We should also be concerned with the spillover effect of economic policies that could go astray if there is political paralysis. The importance of big emerging markets is that they are big, and adverse events in one market can undermine many others. A crisis in Brazil, or Indonesia, or South Africa would have global reverberations, in the same way that it did in Mexico in 1995. Only in these cases, Uncle Sam is not on the border and a rescue operation would be even more difficult to mount. If the big emerging markets as a group slowed their reforms, the pace of world trade would be dramatically curtailed. Indeed, so significant is the Big Ten's position in world trade that a sharp, generalized slowdown in the Big Ten could lead to a global recession.

The Case of India

India is a good example of the explosive mix of political and economic change. The stakes are high because many U.S. firms are banking on the Indian market. India is big enough to transmit its own economic problems throughout South Asia. In addition, economic and political instability in a nuclear power would be extremely worrisome.

While the Indian government is a highly developed democracy, the nation also faces daunting economic challenges, ranging from overcoming its crushing poverty to establishing modern regulations for its banking, stockbroking, and insurance sectors. India began to open up its economy to the world just a few years ago, and it has made a good deal of progress in dropping trade barriers and accommodating some foreign investors. Big American businesses, including General Electric, AT&T, and Coca-Cola, are excited about the future possibilities, because they see for the first time a chance to enter this huge market. But India has barely embarked on the course it must if it is to modernize. Its roads, ports, telecommunications, and airports are appalling. It hasn't enough energy-generating capacity to modernize, and some 25 percent of all energy transmission is lost because of leakages from the existing system. Its agricultural system results in a 30-percent spoilage rate. Its financial system is in need of extensive overhaul. The easy reforms have been taken or are on the drawing boards. But the next generation of reforms will be very difficult.

In mid-1996 India held elections. The long-ruling Congress Party—seen as old, ossified, and corrupt—was replaced by a coalition of thirteen parties, representing every stratum of Indian society. The likelihood of such a fractured group pressing hard for economic reforms, for a reduction of subsidies, for less spending on consumption and more on long-term investment, or for further trade liberalization—all at a pace and on the order of magnitude required—is very slim. For the next few years, the prospect for economic reform is modest and much too little for India's modernization and for U.S. interests. The likelihood is that there will be a slowing down of opportunities for American firms, growing political tension in India, possibly leading to heightened nationalism, and greater difficulty for Washington to influence New Delhi to cooperate with the United States on the world stage.

The Indian case shows the tension between democracy, which fosters equality of participation, and free market economics, which creates great disparity of outcomes. In India the voters said that the reforms of the previous administration were not reaching enough people.

On one of my trips to New Delhi for the Clinton administration, I caught a glimpse of this dilemma. Secretary Brown and I were meeting with the Indian prime minister, P. V. Narashima Rao. We were loaded with briefing books on the full range of issues that Washington always brings up with India—from intellectual property rights to child labor to nuclear nonproliferation. After the opening pleasantries, Rao pointed to the books next to me and said, "Let's not talk about what's in those books. I know those issues. But for this meeting, I have a simple question: How can I explain to the Indian people why the economic reforms that we have taken, and which the world has been applauding, are not reaching many of the Indian people? What can I say?"

Frankly, everything we said sounded as if it came from a textbook. Brown was very frank; no one, he said, had all the answers, and we ourselves had to continually address these issues in the United States.

Several months later, a new and more populist government took over. Although much of the rhetoric gave the appearance that economic reforms would continue, in fact the first official budgets showed that most of the hard economic decisions, such as reducing government expenditures, were being postponed.

The Case of Mexico

The stakes in Mexico's becoming a democratic and economically prosperous country are enormous for the United States because of the growing interaction of our two societies. If Mexico achieves steady economic growth, there will be exceptional opportunities for American firms. The alternative is shrinking markets, more illegal immigration, and more border problems ranging from illegal drug trafficking to environmental degradation.

Like India, Mexico has made impressive economic progress, even despite its recent crisis. In the 1990s, Mexico has moved from being one of the most closed economies to one of the most open, becoming both a major exporter and importer, selling off many of its state-owned firms, and continuing to drop barriers to foreign investment. After a severe recession in 1995, during which Mexico's growth turned sharply negative, GDP expansion in 1996 was estimated at 4 percent and many experts forecast an even stronger performance for 1997.

Now economic liberalization has a political counterpart. While no one would claim that the Institutional Revolutionary Party (P. R.I.) of Mexico, which has ruled with an iron fist for over sixty years, constitutes a true democracy, the system is finally loosening up, with more political accommodation being made to opposition parties. In the summer of 1996, for example, Mexico's government signed an agreement with the opposition parties to eliminate electoral fraud and to modernize the entire political system to make it more responsive to popular opinions. This was seen as the most radical overhaul of the political system since the P. R.I. took power in 1929. Although the lower house in Mexico's Congress reversed some of the measures just a few months later, it appears that opposition candidates now stand a better chance to win key local elections. Moreover, there is widespread agreement that major change is essential if economic reforms are to continue; the country needs a safety valve for the mounting frustration, and it needs a political system that tries harder to meet the needs of the population. The fact is, economic reforms have become painful for most Mexicans, resulting in sky-high unemployment, declining wages, and increased poverty. The degree of income inequality in Mexico, to take one indicator, is growing more extreme. Even the Mexican government admits that 22 million people, some 25 percent of the population, live in extreme poverty, with 5 million people added to that category in the previous fifteen months alone.

In Mexico, economic change has forced political change, but the forces of democracy are extremely chaotic. There used to be many unwritten rules for how the authoritarian government functioned. These are breaking down, but new laws are not in place, creating a dangerous vacuum. Corruption, violence, and confusion are filling the void.

Over time, a democratic capitalist society will serve Mexico and its northern neighbor as well. But over the next several years it is doubtful whether more democracy will produce the desired result, for the transition from an oligarchy to something more democratic may well result in a much slower pace of economic reform, as has occurred in India. There is also the strong possibility that the egalitarian impulses of a democracy, particularly one with so many pent-up frustrations, may give rise to more populist and protectionist policies. What *is* certain is that a dramatic internal struggle among powerful Mexican constituencies is in train, with prospects for political and economic turbulence for years to come.

The Case of Indonesia

Indonesia also illustrates the tensions that result when economic progress outstrips political development. Geographically, this country may seem far away, but instability there will be of immediate concern to the United States because of our enormous economic and political stake in Southeast Asia. If Indonesia has trouble, it would be transmitted throughout the region in the form of political tensions and financial setbacks, so interconnected has the ASEAN group become.

Indonesia has been ruled by a dictator since the 1950s. Economic progress in recent years has been impressive, and now a burgeoning middle class is clamoring for more democracy. "The problem," said an Indonesian economist, "is that while our economy is going global, our politics is still in the era of 'Jurassic Park.'" As in Mexico, the extremes are mind-boggling. Jakarta is generating more than its share of millionaires, and yet the average factory wage in the nation hovers around $3 to $4 a day, and the average civil servant's salary is $45 per month.

In the summer of 1996 there were significant political protests and rioting, of a kind that has not been seen in the last thirty years of tight control over politics and public expression. The government and the people are on a collision course. The country could be in for a long period of instability, since there is no democratic mechanism for choosing a successor to seventy-five-year-old President Suharto. And if there is political turmoil, the Indonesian economy will be in deep trouble because it has become so dependent on foreign investors and lenders for its continued growth, and these financiers will have little stomach for such turmoil.

The Case of South Africa

Just two years ago, South Africa managed a far-reaching transition from an apartheid society to one based on democracy. Alongside these political changes came a commitment to dismantle the economic controls that had underpinned the economy. The changeover was a cause for jubilation, not just in South Africa but around the world.

Today the mood is more sober. In September 1996, *Business Week* quoted a report from the Johannesburg Institute for Defense saying that South Africa "teeters on the brink of becoming simply another African basket case where violence, corruption and brutality rule." A survey in the usually staid *Financial Times* said that the country was "teetering on the edge of anarchy and recession, or at best a steady decline towards permanent third world status . . ." It was not necessary to believe just the press, because foreign investors seemed to agree. In the first ten months of 1996, the value of the South African currency, the rand, dropped by over 20 percent.

The new South African government has promised prosperity and social justice. The first requires fiscal discipline and open markets. The second needs a highly developed democracy. But in the eyes of most of the population—30 percent of whom are unemployed—conventional policies of capitalism will only make the rich better off, while not improving the sad condition of others, and the political system is not coping with the problem. Meanwhile, frustration is building. The criminal justice system cannot stop rising crime. Corruption is widespread, including in the police forces. The need to finance massive education and training of the unskilled black labor force is extremely costly. Skilled white businessmen and professionals continue to leave the country. On top of all this, Nelson Mandela, whose stature and moral authority to govern are unequaled, is due to step down in 1999.

There are other examples where economics and politics collide. China faces a wrenching political transition, and it's anyone's guess whether it will be peaceful or bloody. Turkey's population, dissatisfied with the free-market tendencies of the former government, elected in 1996 its first Islamic government, a highly populist move with likely adverse implications for Western-style economic progress. Brazil's economic reforms, particularly with regard to trade and privatization, are slowing because of populism in the Brazilian congress and also because the ruling officials realize that in order to get reelected they will have to ease up on the economic reforms. Poland may have a major problem finding work for the 2 million workers coming on stream in the next five years, and it will be wrestling with enormous pension obligations of the one-third of the electorate who now receive payments from the government. Argentina also has an acute jobs problem, as unemployment has grown from 6 percent to 18 percent over the last few years. New democracies will be tested by such enormous economic and social pressures.

———

It is not easy to conceive of a more explosive mix—ten countries which are gaining power but which will also be wracked by recurrent instability. The combination of strength and weakness is sure to result in behavior that is erratic and seemingly irrational, and also in enormous headaches for America. Time and again we will be tempted to condemn the actions of individual BEMs for failing to conform to our own neat models about how democracy and free markets go hand in hand. We will talk about containing certain BEMs that will try to use political or military assertiveness as a way to divert the attention of their citizens from the problems at home. The United States will need a long-term strategy to deal with these challenges—plus a lot of patience and diplomatic skill. The U.S. Congress and public will also need a greater awareness of the more complicated global arena that is arising if administration policies are to be supported.

5 Clashes with American Values: Labor Practices, Human Rights, Environmental Protection

Three sources of rising tensions between America and the big emerging markets are fair labor practices, human rights, and environmental protection.

In most cases there is considerable agreement on the values themselves. The problems arise in implementing standards in the context of different societies at varying stages of economic and political development.

Nevertheless, American disappointment about progress on these issues will adversely affect our most basic perceptions of the BEMs, coloring many other aspects of our ties with them.

WHEN HE WAS FIRST campaigning for the presidency in 1992, Bill Clinton criticized President George Bush for being soft on China's human rights record. Clinton pointed to the Bush administration's willingness to allow Beijing to enjoy the same low American tariffs as other countries, rather than using the threat of revoking those privileges as a lever to force China to improve the treatment of its citizens. When he came into office, Clinton promised that when the annual congressional review took place over whether China should be granted an extension of existing trading arrangements—called most favored nation status (MFN)—China would lose its privileges unless there was a clear improvement on the human rights front.

It was a very public threat, and as the June 1994 congressional deadline approached, the administration's mind was concentrated on the critical importance of the decision. In fact, at that time it was impossible to point to any fundamental changes in China's environment for human rights. This resulted in an agonizing dilemma. On the one hand, here was the biggest of the big emerging markets, and American firms were obsessed with entering the country and gaining market share. Many of the Fortune 100 had placed huge bets on China, investing hundreds of millions of dollars to set up offices, hire people, develop strategic plans, and pursue commercial contracts. If Washington were to revoke MFN, China was threatening retaliation against American companies' operations, including those of United Technologies, Westinghouse, and General Electric. On the other hand, the administration did not want to weaken its human rights policy and it did not want to be seen as backing down because of China's threats. It felt its credibility was at stake, not just in China but everywhere, for many other Asian nations were carefully watching whether the United States would make good on its threats.

Secretary Brown and I found ourselves on the front line of the internal administration debate because the Department of Commerce was a key interface between American companies and the administration. Brown hosted several confidential sessions of top corporate leaders, during which there were frank and informal discussions of the pressures acting on the administration. In all the time I have spent in Washington, in four administrations, I saw no issue which raised more concern and emotion in the business community than the tying of trade to human rights in China. Not only were business leaders totally united, with no nuanced differences that I could see, but they were passionate in arguing that the United States was heading down a dangerous path in confronting China or any such powerful country over human rights. No one argued against the cause of human rights; it was what they regarded as the highly public and heavy-handed approach that the executives feared.

Not surprisingly, the Department of Commerce sided with the business community, as did the Treasury. But so did the Defense

Department, which argued that withdrawing MFN would reduce our influence with Beijing across the board. No one had any illusions that dealing with China would be smooth or easy, but Defense was convinced that we needed to push cooperation whenever we could, including in the military arena, and not allow human rights policy to jeopardize it all.

In the end, President Clinton did make a dramatic change in policy, decoupling MFN from human rights. He made the argument that we needed to pursue *both* commercial and human rights goals, but not link them legally. It was an agonizing decision, one which was greeted with dismay and charges of cynicism and hypocrisy by many in Congress, human rights groups, and many important editorial boards. It was a decision which epitomized starkly the dilemmas and trade-offs that we face in dealing with the Big Ten.

———

The United States has always seen itself as a nation that adheres to the highest standards of human rights. Our country's mythology may gloss over the several long and dark periods of our history, but we nevertheless have always believed that we are a human rights model for the world. We have sent our missionaries to the remote corners of the globe to project our notion of how societies should be run. Our presidents, congressmen, and other leaders have preached the human rights gospel from any podium they could find. We have regarded with disdain nations that do not grant maximum freedom to their citizens for free expression and free choice. The fear of contaminating ourselves by dealing with such countries was a major reason for America's chronic isolationist impulse. Very often we have made human rights the leading edge of our foreign policy, even with formidable adversaries like the former Soviet Union. Now comes the most difficult human rights situation that we have faced so far. For it involves not just one country, nor one region, but many countries, the most important of which are the big emerging markets.

Values in Big Emerging Markets Are Often Different

Most other countries have cultures that differ from ours. Europe comes closest to America's self-definition of its own way of life, but even with countries like France and Germany there are significant differences. Virtually no other society places so much importance on individual liberty and legal protection of individual rights as does the United States. In most other nations, much more emphasis is given to stability, order, and community cohesion. But then our country was born in truly unique circumstances. American settlers left a world that was intolerant. Not having a history of feudalism, we did not inherit a rigid, class-ridden society. And there was lots of open space, which allowed Americans enormous freedom to live as they wished.

The farther away we get from Europe, the more national cultures diverge from ours. Sometimes the divergence is less in the words that are said or even in the genuine goals that are put forward but in the actual practice. In all the big emerging markets, for example, most officials will support human rights goals, but often their first priority is political order. Some believe that economic growth will improve the human rights situation, others that human rights must come second. In Asia, some believe that rampant individualism is a Western vice, and at odds with the kind of communitarianism that exists in that part of the world. And most big emerging markets lack adequate governmental means to enforce human rights laws.

During the Cold War, Washington often subordinated human rights goals to overriding strategic interests. Because of Iran's strategic position in the Middle East, for example, we maintained close ties with the Shah of Iran at a time when his regime was repressive and torture was a widespread practice. In the future our policy makers will find much less political flexibility at home to downplay human rights issues because of geopolitical interests. In a world that is becoming more intertwined as a result of trade, travel, and telecommunications, the differences in values held by so many emerging markets will become more apparent to Americans. The media, with instant global reach, will bring these issues into our kitchens and living rooms. They will be a major sticking point with Congress, with labor unions, and with the growing number of well-organized, politically connected human rights organizations. As a result, differences in the way people are treated in other countries are bound to create serious clashes in our relationships—clashes which have implications for trade, foreign policy, and the activities of our companies around the world.

LABOR STANDARDS

Americans are becoming more conscious of labor standards abroad, and they often recoil at what they see. Two types of issues will receive much more attention. The first is low wage rates abroad, which is already being identified as the cause of rising imports into the United States as well as the reason why American companies are transferring their operations abroad. But there is a second dimension to labor standards which is often more offensive to Americans. These relate not to how much foreign workers are paid, but how they are treated. In the new international vocabulary, these are called "core labor standards," and they embody three objectives: no exploitation of child labor; no slavery or forced labor; and the allowance of free speech, free association, and collective bargaining. There is a clear connection between these core standards and wages in that the standards have an impact on *how* wage rates are determined. But beyond that, there are significant moral issues relating to the harsh and degrading ways in which human beings are treated.

And these issues won't go away. Take the use of child labor. The International Labor Organization estimates that about 250 million children under the age of fourteen are working in developing countries, nearly three times previous estimates. A recent report indicates that 24 percent of children work in Turkey, 16 percent in Brazil, 14 percent in India, 11 percent in China, 10 percent in Indonesia, 7 percent in Mexico.

A few specific examples: In Indonesia laws are a mishmash of prohibitions and exceptions. Child labor is prohibited generally, but it is allowed frequently for "socioeconomic" reasons—a broad exemption in a country of nearly 200 million people, most of them very poor. There are no reliable statistics, and no employers have ever been taken to court for violations of the statutes.

In India, the constitution prohibits employment of children under fourteen years of age, and yet the Indian government estimates that there are 17.5 million children working, the International Labor Organization estimates 44 million, and nongovernmental organizations estimate 55 million.

In Brazil, there are credible reports of forced labor in many parts of the country. The government itself admits that its capability to enforce labor laws is totally inadequate. Labor organizations in the country allege that thousands of workers are hired on the basis of false promises and that they are subject to debt bondage and forced prostitution, and retained by the use of violence.

In Indonesia free assembly is frequently prohibited under laws that interpret public demonstrations of many kinds as threats to the state itself.

Labor and Trade

In recent years the International Labor Organization has tried to call attention to abuses in all three categories, but progress has been very slow. The United States, along with several European nations, also wants to bring the question of core labor standards into the trade arena. Washington's goal is to put pressure on emerging markets to end abhorrent labor practices by adding new rules to the charter of the World Trade Organization. Were this to happen, there would also be penalties in the form of higher tariffs on products originating from countries violating the new standards.

Not surprisingly, China, the ASEAN group, and others flatly reject this approach. It used to be that trade battles were over tariffs, quotas, and subsidies. Now they will be over how countries treat their workers. Major trading partners going head to head over such sensitive domestic issues will not be a pretty sight. The entire trading system could be disrupted.

Tying labor standards so explicitly to trade will cause problems for Washington. Wielding such a stick seems based on an outmoded concept that others need us more than we need them. In practice, we will be very reluctant to sanction China, as recent history has shown. With the ASEAN group, we would likely encounter the very same problem, that our interests in continuing trade—indeed in expanding it—are paramount. There are difficult trade-offs that Washington will have to balance extremely carefully.

This much is for sure: Attempts to implant American idealism will encounter very rough winds. Most big emerging market leaders believe that America is merely clothing protectionism in the guise of morality. They argue that the United States cannot stop competitive imports except by appealing to the idealistic impulse of Americans. They are thus opposed to serious dialogue with Washington on these issues for both economic and political reasons.

Beyond that, however, these are knotty issues, often more gray than black and white. In most of the Big Ten, the intention to improve the situation exists. The presidents of Mexico, Brazil, and South Africa, for example, have been eloquent in articulating the need for better treatment of workers. It is the pressure of poverty and the lack of a strong capability to enforce laws that make it so difficult to bring humane treatment up to our modern standards. There is often a genuine belief that with economic progress, working conditions will improve, and that America is trying to impose the values of a modern society on societies that are still emerging.

BROADER HUMAN RIGHTS

While an intense U.S. preoccupation with labor standards is relatively new, a focus on broader human rights abuses overseas is not. American concerns go back many decades, but official government responsibility was formalized in 1976 with legislation charging the State Department to establish a division of human rights, a human rights coordinator, and procedures to investigate and formally report on the conditions for human rights in virtually every country. Today there is an Assistant Secretary of State for Democracy, Human Rights, and Labor charged—as the title indicates—with a very broad mandate.

Since the late 1970s, Washington has mounted an intense effort to publicize human rights abuses abroad. The State Department's annual reports detail such developments as extrajudicial killings, disappearances, torture, arbitrary arrests, denial of fair trials, interference in free expression, and discrimination based on race, sex, religion—as well as the abrogation of core labor standards. Indeed, the 1995 human rights report makes depressing reading. China is accused of arbitrary and lengthy incommunicado detention, of torture and mistreatment of prisoners, of restrictions on free speech, the press, religion. Turkey was accused, among other violations, of abusing its antiterrorism law to harass, intimidate, and imprison human rights monitors, journalists, and lawyers. India, it was said, was guilty of all manner of crimes against people in police custody, including rape and torture. Brazil, too, had a very bad record when it came to police brutality.

Some Specific Cases: Turkey, Brazil, Indonesia

Several specific cases illustrate that human rights problems are deeply rooted in the fundamental history and politics of a society. Each has become a long-standing conflict, publicized by human rights groups and the press. The significance of these cases includes indescribable human suffering, of course. But they also go to the heart of American relations with several of the BEMs, revealing not just the dilemmas we face in balancing commercial interests with human rights concerns, but the particularly long-standing and deep-seated nature of the human rights problems themselves, and the difficulty of eradicating them within a short time frame. Critics of U.S. policy who say that Washington should condition relations on human rights often ignore the fact that the situations are not a question of several dissidents being rounded up and imprisoned, horrible as that may be. The problem often relates to perceived threats to national security.

In Turkey, a big problem concerns the clash between the Turkish military and the Kurdistan Workers Party (PKK), whose goal is a separate state of Kurdistan in southeastern Turkey. The Turkish government considers the PKK to be a terrorist organization which is trying to mount an insurrection. In 1987 Ankara declared a state of emergency in ten southeastern provinces. The civilian authorities were given powers akin to martial law, and the Turkish armed forces have taken on the role of internal security. By all accounts the military faces an intractable situation of internal terrorism. Nevertheless, according to reports by U.S. government and human rights groups, the army systematically uses excessive force, including forced evacuation and burning of villages and torture of prisoners held in detention. In addition, people representing human rights groups, journalists, and others expressing ideas counter to Ankara's policy are harassed and intimidated by Turkish government officials. In a report released in September 1996, Amnesty International said that more than one thousand civilians suspected of pro-rebel activity had been killed since 1991 "in an unprecedented wave of extrajudicial killings."

Brazil represents a much different kind of human rights problem. In 1985 military government gave way to democratic elections for the first time in two decades. The criminal justice system was returned to civilian control. However, the requirements for a modern system of law enforcement have not been met, and the situation is getting worse. One source of pressure is the grinding poverty in Brazil, a country with one of the most unequal patterns of income and wealth in the world. On top of this is rapid urbanization: Between 1964 and 1994 the population in Brazil's cities escalated from 34.9 million to 114.9 million, leading to massive unemployment and millions living without the most basic services.

The conditions for frustration and crime—colliding with a police force whose legacy is military rule and which is totally unprepared to cope with lawlessness—has created a national crisis. State police are frequently implicated in killings and abuse of prisoners, not to mention vigilante lynchings of suspected criminals, or execution-style killing of street children. The courts are overloaded and rarely investigate police brutality. The poor are victimized routinely, and there are recurrent reports of massacres of landless peasants.

President Fernando Henrique Cardoso, who has a long record of activism in favor of protection of human rights, has backed legislation to strengthen humane law enforcement. There have been numerous commissions and investigations into police violence. But the problems run very deep in the political and socioeconomic culture. In March 1995, for example, police in Rio de Janeiro apprehended a robber outside of a pharmacy. He was dragged behind a police van and summarily executed. The incident was captured on TV and played back across the nation. Polls showed the majority of Rio's residents approved of the killing, so great was their frustration with rising crime.

Indonesia illustrates another human rights debacle. East Timor, the eastern half of an island about 1,300 miles east of Jakarta, was a part of Portugal's overseas colonies. In 1974 Lisbon's empire collapsed when Portugal turned from military dictatorship to democracy. Indonesia had sovereignty in the western portion of Timor, and proceeded to annex the eastern part. The international community never recognized the conquest. According to human rights groups and the U.S. government, Indonesia has maintained a brutal occupation of East Timor, including harsh repression of dissidents, arbitrary arrests and detentions, restrictions on civil liberties, and harassment of critics of the Indonesian government. There are numerous instances of kidnappings and disappearances. Human rights groups estimate that some 200,000 East Timorese, or one-third of the population, have died as a result of the Indonesian forces' activities in the last two decades. The government of Indonesia, while not giving way to international criticism, has nevertheless invited human rights experts to visit East Timor and allowed the establishment of a National Human Rights Commission.

Resentment Against U.S. Pressure

America's detailed accusations of human rights abuses run head on into the most fundamental national sensitivities of other countries. Many human rights issues are seen as life-and-death matters for the BEM governments. In addition, the unleashing of market forces, and the pressures for democratization, decentralization, and government downsizing mean that the central governments of the Big Ten are losing power, not gaining it, even as their police forces and their legal systems are in severe need of the kind of modernization that only strong government can provide. It will, therefore, be a long time before violations of human rights are reduced to a level that is even remotely comparable to what we consider acceptable in the West or Japan. Meanwhile, these abuses will remain in our consciousness because they will be highlighted in our popular magazines and on our TV screens. And they will increasingly color our ties with countries that are growing in importance to us.

Not surprisingly, many big emerging markets deeply resent what they see as America's highhandedness in so publicly preaching the gospel of human rights. In Asia, in particular, a backlash is brewing. China is adamantly opposed to U.S. public accusations. It seems that the louder we talk, the more dissidents Beijing tends to round up. The ASEAN group is also fed up and increasingly defiant. In the summer of 1996, when the United States objected to ASEAN's welcoming Burma—with its repressive military regime—

into its membership, the Asians' first reaction was to tell us to get lost. In fact, our strident warnings may have had the opposite effect to what we intended. When, at the same time, Washington condemned the repression of Indonesian political opposition, the reaction was the same. Americans may feel good about publicly highlighting abuses, and we may feel bound to shout our feelings from the rooftops, but the effectiveness of such a policy within the BEMs themselves is another question.

In recent years, the challenge to Western values has taken the form of Asian leaders talking about "Asian values" and differentiating them from our own. Singapore's most important statesman, Lee Kwan Yew, and Malaysia's prime minister, Mohamad Mahathir, have been exponents of Asia's difference, pointing to the emphasis on community, order, and consensus in their region. Mahathir has gone as far as saying that "European values are European values; Asian values are universal values." The rising consciousness in Asia that there is, in fact, another way to organize society—combined with the obvious economic success of Asian nations—is a powerful force, and will add to polarization between the United States and Asia. This standoff is likely to get more acute in the near term because of the growing assertiveness of several BEMs and the lack of visible allies to help the United States press its cause—at least in the way we are pursuing it.

The Global Environment

In recent years the international agenda of political leaders has included issues that were not always considered high priorities for the United States—certainly not on a par with military preparedness or trade. But as the world shrinks, problems abroad can spill over into our own country and our own lifestyles, and can be addressed successfully only if the United States and other countries work together closely. These challenges include terrorism, narcotics trafficking, population pressures, and environmental protection. America's relations with the big emerging markets will have to address all of these issues. We may seek to curb the illegal drug trade with Mexico's assistance, for example, or try to isolate terrorist states by enlisting the help of Turkey.

The interrelated questions of population pressure and the environment provide a particularly good example of both the opportunities and tensions that the big emerging markets will create.

Within the next twenty-five years, the world's population is projected to grow by 42 percent—from its current 5.7 billion to 8.1 billion—and virtually all of this growth will occur in the developing world. By the year 2025, China, India, Indonesia, and Brazil alone will account for 45 percent of the world's population. Most of the big emerging markets will increase their populations by 60 percent, whereas the number of people in Europe and Japan will hardly grow at all.

While no one knows for sure what the real implications of this trend will be, some educated guesses can be made. Unchecked population pressures are likely to aggravate poverty. Cities in the big emerging markets will grow to unprecedented size. For example, São Paulo could encompass a population of 25 million, Bombay 24 million, Mexico City 18 million, Jakarta 17 million. Pressures of so many people will put unbearable strains on transportation, water, shelter. Civil violence, especially between ethnic groups, may grow. The situation for human rights and labor will get worse. Every aspect of the environment will deteriorate. These kinds of pressures will surely complicate America's objective of creating democracies and free markets.

The broader environmental question looms especially large. Because of their size, their growing industrialization, and the urgency they attach to business expansion and job creation, most big emerging markets have barely begun to put in place effective environmental programs. They haven't the money, the skilled management, nor—in their minds—the luxury of dealing with the environment at this stage of their development. They lack financing capability, too, especially in light of competing priorities such as transportation systems, power generation, and housing. It will be impossible, however, for the West to deal with questions like climate change, deforestation, or resource depletion without the cooperation of China, India, Brazil, and some of the others, but seeking this kind of relationship amidst all the other tensions will be hard.

ENVIRONMENTAL PROBLEMS IN CHINA, BRAZIL, AND POLAND

China plans to construct more than one hundred new power plants in the next decade, most of which will burn coal. During the 1990s, China's annual use of coal is expected to increase by 40 percent to approximately 1.4 billion metric tons, roughly one-third of annual worldwide production. In addition, the country's automobile industry will devour billions of gallons of gasoline without the pollution safeguards known in the West. The combined effect of dependence on coal and demand for gasoline will not only have severe global consequences. Within five years, China is projected to account for 75 percent of East Asia's sulfur dioxide emissions. China is now the third largest contributor to global climate changes, after the United States and Russia. By the mid-twenty-first century, if current trends continue, China could be the biggest culprit.

Another significant impact of BEMs on the environment concerns the tropical rainforests in Brazil, which have been disappearing at an alarming rate. As a result the local ecosystem is threatened, leading to soil erosion, depletion of soil productivity, and drying up of the waterways. In addition, three-quarters of the plant and animal species in the rainforest have disappeared, causing significant damage to the global ecosystem. And in recent years, epidemiologists have begun to suspect that the human devastation of tropical environments may have contributed to the unleashing some of the world's "killer" viruses, including Ebola and yellow fever.

Poland reflects the impact of rampant industrialization without environmental consciousness—a result of being behind the Iron Curtain for over four decades. Saddled with an old and inefficient industrial infrastructure, Poland has been using three times more energy per unit of industrial output than her Western European neighbors. Most Polish factories and power plants lack all but rudimentary pollution-control equipment; in 1993 experts estimated that providing Polish industry with modern environmental equipment could cost nearly $10 billion. As a result, Poland's problems are not only its own, but Europe's. Its pollution of the atmosphere knows few national boundaries, causing acid rain across the continent.

ENVIRONMENT AND TRADE

It is safe to say that these demographic and environmental problems will occupy center stage on international negotiating agendas for decades to come. But they are trade-related problems, as well. From the U.S. perspective, the argument often goes like this: "Isn't it unfair if companies from Mexico or India or Turkey can produce products to sell to us without having to invest in pollution control just as American companies must? Isn't it an unfair price advantage?"

How are the United States and the big emerging markets going to handle these issues? A straw in the wind is the way that environmental issues have already been dealt with in the trading arena. In the NAFTA negotiations, the United States insisted on Mexico's commitments to implement its environmental laws. They were the first such environmental arrangements in any trade agreement. The treaty almost collapsed over this issue, because Congress wanted more stringent provisions and Mexico didn't want any. But the American view prevailed.

A year later Washington took the lead in saying that the World Trade Organization ought to examine the environmental issue with the possibility of linking trade to it. A logical next step in this line of reasoning was that countries who did not adhere to environmental obligations of the WTO—once they were in place—would be subject to higher tariffs or to trade sanctions. Emerging markets saw this thrust as straight protectionism and they vehemently opposed it. This dispute may prove to be the opening salvo in what promises to be one of the central trade issues of the next decade.

We can say for sure that America must somehow engage in the big geopolitical game, in reinforcing the efforts of nations trying to establish the foundations of democracy and free markets, and in advocating and defending the values we hold dear. But we have no experience on which to rely, in trying to figure out how much outside pressure works and how much produces a backlash; whether private pressure behind the scenes is better than public condemnation; or how to best balance all the interests we have with big emerging markets—economic, political, security, human rights, and environmental. What *can* be said with confidence is that we do need a new framework for thinking about these problems, one that takes account of how the BEMs are evolving, what the thinking of their leaders and citizens is, and what America's role in this new world should be. It is to that task that we now turn, first with a discussion of why we are not well prepared to deal with the future, and then with some thoughts of what we must do.

6 America Unprepared

American history has not prepared us to meet the challenges of the big emerging markets.

Nor is congressional or American public opinion ready to deal with the upcoming challenges, because we are turning inward at precisely the time we need to be more engaged in the world.

False optimism regarding how well our nation is doing at present could also catch us way off guard.

I HAD A HUMBLING EXPERIENCE concerning my own vision of America during a two-week business trip through Asia while in the Clinton administration. During a stop in Singapore the American embassy had arranged a lunch for me with about a dozen young Singaporean men and women who were likely future leaders. Some worked in large companies, some were entrepreneurs, some came from government agencies, some from think tanks. The discussion began with where Singapore was headed, then turned to the personal dreams of the Singaporean participants, but ultimately centered on their views of the United States and American leadership. I heard a lot about their admiration for my country, but I was taken aback by their understanding of our shortcomings, too.

For example, they questioned me on why we Americans look down on lawlessness in many parts of the world, when by so many measures—homicides, larcenies, rape—we are among the most violent societies on earth. They recognized the tragedy of young children being forced to work, but asked how we rationalized the fact that over 20 percent of American children live in poverty. They understood why the United States pushes hard for open markets abroad or for stronger protection of intellectual property rights, but referred to America's early history, when it was an emerging market and followed a policy of high protective tariffs and regularly pirated British publications.

Listening to these feelings, which were expressed in a very sincere and low-key manner, I recalled similar encounters during my travels in Brazil, Argentina, India, and China. It caused me to think that as great a nation as we are, we harbor an unrealistic view that everyone wants to be like us. This gap between the way we see ourselves and how others see us is likely to get wider as a new and more confident generation takes up leadership positions in the BEMs. They will have only dim memories of America's accomplishments during the Cold War and much more pride in the achievements of their own societies. It is not that millions of people abroad do not envy the liberties that Americans have. They no doubt do. But the entire American package is not always as attractive as we think it is. Americans need a more realistic and balanced perspective of how others see us these days, and we need to be better prepared to work with leaders in the BEMs who are not so quick to say the American way is the only way.

———

For starters, our own history is not a good guide for how we should think about engaging the Big Ten in the future.

Ever since the War of Independence, our nation has been uncomfortable with most forms of foreign involvement. Our effort to stay aloof from foreign affairs is due partly to the way the early settlers in America turned their backs on Europe and eventually declared independence. In the view of many colonial leaders, America was to be different than any other nation—more open, more democratic, more righteous. We were to be "the city on the hill," an example for others to view from afar and to emulate. Our influence was to be passive. The political and economic experiment on these shores, so the philosophy went, was a unique experiment that would be "contaminated" if America involved itself with the Old World governments and their more authoritarian political systems, their disregard for popular opinion, and their political scheming on the world stage.

In one way or another, our foreign policy has always embodied this reluctance to engage in the traditional game of international diplomacy and power politics, even as times have changed. The big debates in our foreign policy—whether to dislodge Spain from Cuba and the Philippines at the turn of the last century, whether to enter either of the two world wars, whether to fight in Vietnam, whether to take on Saddam Hussein—all revolved around the balance between perceived threats to our security versus the costs of foreign involvement. Those costs were measured in lives, to be sure, but also in terms of distraction from problems at home, and of the damage to our democracy if the federal government were to seize the kinds of controls necessary to conduct an active foreign policy—be it conscription, higher taxes, or excessive use of secrecy in dealing with foreign governments or its own citizens.

PRESIDENTS AND GLOBAL INVOLVEMENT

A quick look at four presidents who had a fundamental and enduring influence on our attitudes toward involvement in world affairs says a lot about ourselves.

George Washington's warning in his farewell address echoes to this day. He said:

> The great rule of conduct for us, in regard to foreign nations, is in extending our commercial relations to have with them as little political connection as possible. So far as we have already formed engagements, let them be fulfilled with perfect good faith. Here let us stop.

Washington went on to say that Europe's interests were different from our own, and he urged his countrymen not to get involved in the scheming politics or the shifting, collusive alliances on the European continent. Why, he asked,

> by interweaving our destiny with that of any part of Europe, [should we] entangle our peace and prosperity in the toils of European ambition, rivalship, interest, humor, or caprice?

Washington's philosophy was endorsed by the nation's third president, Thomas Jefferson, who underscored the uniqueness of America's situation and her view of herself. Our job, said Jefferson, was to focus on the special democratic experiment at home. We had the luxury, by virtue of geography, to do it and to avoid being contaminated by the outside world.

> Let us, then, with courage and confidence pursue our own Federal and Republican principles, our attachment to union and representative government. Kindly separated by nature and a wide ocean from the exterminating havoc of one-quarter of the globe . . . possessing a chosen country with room enough for our descendants to the hundredth and thousandth generation . . . with all these blessings, what more is necessary to make us a happy and prosperous people?

The Washington–Jefferson outlook was embraced by all of their successors for most of the nineteenth century, as America stayed aloof from foreign political entanglements. The United States focused instead on developing its political system and its economy, expanding westward to the Pacific Ocean, and holding the nation together in the face of a bloody civil war.

It was not until the close of the century that the attention of some leaders turned toward the outside world, where an imperial scramble for colonies was taking place, and where England, France, Germany, Russia, Japan, and others were angling to expand their power, territory, and markets. A new view was emerging about America's proper role in the world, personified by Theodore Roosevelt, who became president in 1901, a time when the United States had become a highly industrialized society with booming financial markets, massive business enterprises, and a transcontinental rail system. Roosevelt envisioned America as a world power, a nation that should not be content to sit on the sidelines while others divided up the globe.

Like the Founding Fathers, Roosevelt felt that America was a unique example to the world. But whereas Washington and Jefferson were content to have the United States a passive example to other nations, Roosevelt advocated an active policy of international involvement, one in which America unilaterally would exercise its will. He wanted to challenge the imperial powers in the Caribbean and in the Pacific. He felt that America should have total freedom of action wherever it so wanted—such as in China, which was in the process of being carved up by England, France, Germany, and Japan. "I wish to see the United States the dominant power in the Pacific Ocean," he wrote in 1900. "Our people are neither cravens nor weaklings and we face the future high of heart and confident of soul, eager to do the great work of a great world power." In fact, Roosevelt abhorred the sentimental philosophy that America's purity would be spoiled by engagement with other governments, viewing America's involvement instead as a way to purify those other nations.

Woodrow Wilson, who took office in 1913, represented another variant of American thinking. Like his predecessors, he felt that America was a shining example to the rest of the world, more righteous than any other nation. Unlike Washington and Jefferson, but like Roosevelt, he was an enthusiastic advocate of active U.S. involvement in international affairs. But he differed from Roosevelt in the nature of that involvement. Roosevelt, after all, wanted to impose American values through the sheer force of her navy and marines and the use of trade embargoes. He wanted not simply to emulate the tactics of the major powers of the time, but to outplay them at their own game. There would be no international coordination or consensus—it would be every nation for itself. Wilson, on the other hand, was a moralist and an idealist about international politics. He dedicated himself to building a new international order, in which power politics and the pursuit of selfish interests were subordinated to a higher level of moral conduct among nations.

For Wilson, America had a moral duty to lift other nations to a higher level of behavior. It could do so by creating and leading a League of Nations that would put an end to war and focus on improving the condition of mankind, liberating oppressed people everywhere. Wilson had a romantically optimistic view of what other nations could become. He felt that they could turn away from their belligerent instincts; set aside their need to acquire more territory, prestige, and power; end their balance-of-power games; and allow their people to determine their own fate through free elections. Wilson saw a clear relationship between America's character at home and its role abroad, a connection he defended in trying to persuade Congress to pass legislation allowing America to join the League of Nations in the months following the end of World War I.

Wilson believed that it was America's duty to provide a vision for the world, and to build a formal set of treaties and arrangements to implement that vision. He once described the age as one "which rejects the standards of national selfishness that once governed the councils of nations and demands that they shall give way to a new order of things in which the only questions will be, 'Is it right? Is it just? Is it in the interest of mankind?' "

AMERICAN EXCEPTIONALISM

All these presidents took as their starting point the unique nature of American society, what historians have called "American exceptionalism." None doubted that our way of life—our system of politics, our economic principles, our cultural values—was the example that other nations ought to follow. The American way could enlighten corrupt people or backward people, bring them religion and morality, bring them democratic political systems and open markets—so the thinking went. Our mission was one of liberating and civilizing. The only differences were those of approach: Should it be by passive example or should we be proactive? And if we were proactive, should we bulldoze our way, or should we create a cooperative council of nations and work within it?

When America entered World War II, the terms of the debate changed somewhat, but not totally. The big difference from previous eras was that for the first time the United States saw its security being threatened by Japan and Germany. After their defeat, the Soviet Union loomed as another, even more serious threat because of its nuclear missiles. Under these circumstances, there was no choice but to set aside George Washington's admonitions and become permanently involved in world politics.

But America remained true to its historic missionary zeal. When President Harry Truman announced his first large foreign aid proposal, a program to help Greece and Turkey fight off Communism, he said in 1947, "It must be the policy of the United States to support free people who are resisting attempted subjugation by armed minorities or by outside pressures." Later, President John F. Kennedy took up the universal mission, saying in his 1961 inaugural that America would "pay any price, bear any burden" in the defense of liberty around the world. Still, the nature of that involvement was always being debated between the disciples of Roosevelt, who wanted to practice power politics, and the Wilsonians, who wanted to place more faith in international bodies like the United Nations.

But it was the Vietnam war that caused Americans to return to some of the concerns of George Washington and Thomas Jefferson. Until this far-off military conflict, in the minds of most Americans there seemed to be no limit as to what the United States could accomplish at home and abroad. But with Vietnam, the basic questions of America's Founding Fathers were posed again: Is this kind of involvement, so tangential to direct threats to our security, going to distract us from problems at home? Is it going to create a government, which, because of the requirements of war, embraces antidemocratic habits such as more secrecy, more political manipulation, and more usurpation of powers that ought not to be in the hands of the executive branch of government? George Washington's advice would certainly have been to stay away from Vietnam. Roosevelt, like presidents Lyndon Johnson and Richard Nixon, would have tried to conquer Vietnam with all of America's power. Wilson would have fought the war for moral reasons—to make sure that democracy didn't lose ground—and he would have tried tirelessly to involve the United Nations.

In the years since Vietnam, there have been few defining debates on foreign policy. American involvement in Nicaragua, Grenada, and Panama became miniature versions of the Vietnam debate, but the stakes and the risks were too small to create great waves of anguish. The Gulf War, even though it lasted only a short while, brought to the fore America's conflicting impulses, and had it not been for a forceful performance by President George Bush, Congress might well have balked at giving its blessing to the sending of U.S. troops. Even after an unambiguous victory, however, Washington did not have the stomach to finish the war by removing Saddam Hussein, and withdrew American forces before the Iraqi regime and its army had collapsed. More recently, the sending of American troops to Somalia and Bosnia was possible only because they were on peacekeeping missions and because the timing of the troops' withdrawal was agreed on at the time they were sent. Congress would certainly not have sanctioned any combat role.

TRADE HAS BEEN DIFFERENT

The pulling and tugging over America's involvement in the world never affected U.S. trade policy in the same way. True, there were major debates between free-market and protectionist groups over tariffs, but to a great extent these followed the normal pattern of a nation that was industrializing. There was a natural desire to protect emerging industries; for most of the nineteenth century, in fact, the United States favored high tariffs. But later, when U.S. firms became powerful enough not just to hold their own but also to exploit foreign markets, there was a push for more open trade around the world. For most of the twentieth century, the Great Depression being an exception, the United States strongly advocated open markets on every continent.

Throughout our history, trade was seen as generally beneficial to the nation. George Washington specifically omitted commercial relations from his warning against political entanglements. Roosevelt did not appear interested in trade for its own sake, but he did see it as an adjunct of American power, and so favored open markets. Woodrow Wilson was particularly passionate about encouraging American trade. He constantly talked of a world order of liberal political and capitalist values and a global system characterized by open trade and world law. He was conscious of the growing commercial prowess of the United States, and saw American penetration of foreign markets not only in our own interest but as a humanitarian service to the world—a fusion of U.S. political and economic goals:

> America has stood in the years past for that sort of political understanding among men which would let every man feel that his rights were the same as those of another, and the mission of America in the field of world commerce is to be the same.

In 1941 President Franklin Roosevelt made free trade an integral part of an early agreement with the allies, the Atlantic Charter, which laid out the values of the post–World War II world. All his successors followed suit. While the benefits of open trade would be debated time and again by various U.S. interest groups—the agriculture lobby, steel, textiles, labor unions—the overall thrust of U.S. policy has not changed. Trade expansion was seen as being in the national interest. There was little fear of contaminating the American economic system even if trade occurred with dictatorships or with countries practicing a different kind of economics. Trade expansion was not equated necessarily with having close political ties with our trading partners.

WHY SO MUCH OF OUR HISTORY IS IRRELEVANT TO THE FUTURE

What does this short, cursory history say about America's preparation to face upcoming global challenges? We can appreciate George Washington's sentiments about engaging in commercial relations but remaining aloof from political engagement. It might have been an appropriate policy for a young country of some 2 million people far from the center of global politics. But since the middle of this century, political isolation has not been a real option for the United States, given our military responsibilities and our vital economic links around the globe.

With respect to trade, the environment is changing dramatically, too. Trade has become—and will remain—more important to the United States than at any time in the last century. As the direct military threats have become less tangible, trade will dominate politics rather than vice versa. It will no longer be possible to say, "We'll trade with China but we won't have intimate political relations." The only way to expand trade is to be dealing with Chinese officials from the president to the foreign minister to the governors and mayors. We will find that trade, and its impact on the Chinese economy and on China's role in the world, is high politics in China itself. Indeed, there and everywhere, trade has become the heart of domestic and global politics.

A reading of our history also shows that the only kind of international engagement that we could sustain involved threats to our national security—threats that were seen as military in nature. When it comes to thinking about our role in the world now, we must refocus. There are no real military threats to our security at this time. But there are a lot of other threats—from lack of foreign markets to terrorism to environmental degradation which spills across borders. We have no real experience in sustaining interest and involvement in those issues.

The formulas of our past presidents will not work in the future. The isolationism of George Washington, the gunboat mentality of Theodore Roosevelt, the excessive moralism of Woodrow Wilson—none of these models is appropriate now. We cannot remain aloof from world politics, because we have too much of a stake in what other nations do. We ought not expend all our energy twisting others' arms, because too many other countries are in a position to successfully resist. And we cannot afford to be too idealistic, because the world is filled with important countries that will dash our hopes and create great disillusionment in our country and a substantial backlash against the kind of involvement we need to maintain.

A final difference from the past is that for most of our history, our sustained foreign engagements have been with Europe and, more recently, with Japan. It has been our consistent objective to create a world order that reflects traditional American values and principles. And while we have never been satisfied, we had the easiest time with Europe, where the traditions were closest to ours, and the hardest time with Japan, where the culture and institutions derived from a much different tradition. Whenever we became heavily involved in the Third World—in Latin America or in Asia, for example—we had an even more difficult time. The upcoming clash of values with big emerging markets will be the most bracing experience of all, testing our tolerance for engagement with countries that are so different from us as that tolerance has never been tested.

American Attitudes Toward the World

It is not easy to identify precisely what American attitudes toward global involvement are, because we are such a diverse country and because there are so many ways—seen and unseen—in which we are engaged with other countries. But we are not well prepared for the kinds of involvements that are in store for us.

One of the most authoritative surveys done on this subject comes from the Chicago Council on Foreign Relations in its most recent "Survey of American Public Opinion and U.S. Foreign Policy." For five years the Council polls American leaders as well as the general public, examining American attitudes about politics, economics, and military relationships. The underlying question is always: To what extent do American leaders and the public support an active role for the United States overseas?

The latest survey, conducted at the end of 1995, supports the contention that Americans are badly prepared to face a changing world. While it reveals that "Americans are committed to an active role for the United States in the world," it also shows that most of us have little understanding about what kind of world it will be. The survey gives a broad picture of a population that sees very little discontinuity in the world. An adjustment here, a modification there, but otherwise "steady as she goes" seems to be the governing philosophy.

For example, when asked to identify America's most important relationships, the general public listed Japan, Saudi Arabia, Russia, Kuwait, Mexico, and Canada. Asked to rate our biggest foreign policy problems, the public gave top priority to "getting involved in other countries," followed by "too much foreign aid" and "too much illegal immigration." When asked to list the problems they see in the country, domestic and foreign, there was plenty of concern about jobs—in fact, the percentage of respondents who rated protecting jobs as a very important part of foreign policy stood at an all-time high. But when asked about how the United States was doing in the world, the public registered significant confidence that Washington was in good control of events, apparently with little anxiety about the commercial challenges we face or the political and economic instabilities that loom so large in the BEMs.

The survey also focused on the opinions of "leaders" from government, business, and nonprofit organizations. The views of these men and women showed a different pattern—more awareness of the BEMs, to be sure, more emphasis on trade, but nothing that evidences the fundamental challenges posed by big emerging markets, nothing that reflects an awareness of the degree of foreign policy involvement that will be required in the future, and nothing that shows an understanding of how global economic affairs have come to the fore. In one telling poll, leaders ranked ten national problems and put foreign policy at the end—after crime, budget deficits, education, immorality, health care, unemployment, racism, dissatisfaction with government, and general economic problems.

Experts will argue whether or not we, as a nation, are turning inward, although I am convinced that we as a society are moving steadily in that direction. But there is certainly *no* basis at all to conclude that we are turning outward at the very time that the challenges from abroad are becoming more relevant to our lives and vastly more complicated than they have been.

PAROCHIAL CONGRESSIONAL VIEWS ON TRADE

Some of these problems were driven home to me in my interactions with Congress after the Republican victory in 1994. In the winter of 1995, the new Congress set as one of its highest priorities the elimination of the Department of Commerce. I spent a good deal of time on Capitol Hill talking to our legislators about their underlying reason for wanting to cut back on the people who handle trade promotion. I explained what we were doing to help Boeing sell aircraft or General Electric to sell turbines, but I also made it clear that we had an even bigger mission of helping small and medium-size firms around the country to get into the world market. We had done our homework, and I could identify specific small companies that Washington had helped in every state in the nation, even with the company's own estimates of the jobs that had been saved, supported, or created. I could show them our calculations indicating how for every dollar of tax money being spent to expand U.S. exports, at least four dollars was being returned to the Treasury as a result of taxes collected on the revenues deriving from exports that were facilitated by Uncle Sam. Why, I asked, would Congress wish to abolish this service, particularly at a time when every major government in the world, from London to Tokyo, was expanding its help to its country's firms? The answers were frequently mind-boggling. Many would ask me why are exports important in the first place? I'm concerned about jobs, not exports, some would say, unable to make any connection between the two. In other cases, Congress would segue into tirades about human rights or illegal immigration as an excuse for why the government shouldn't be involved in exporting to certain countries at all. And so it went.

SHORT-SIGHTED ATTITUDES TO FINANCING INTERNATIONAL INSTITUTIONS AND AMERICAN EMBASSIES

Trade promotion wasn't the only area in which Congress revealed its parochial attitudes. In the last few years the United States has continued its trend to renege on commitments made to international organizations. By mid-1996, for example, the United States was in arrears of $500 million to the United Nations for normal budget operations, $600 million for peacekeeping operations, and many more millions to affiliated U.N. agencies like the World Health Organization and the Food and Agriculture Organization. Although we have been giving less foreign aid as a percentage of our GDP than any other industrial country, our foreign aid levels have continued to decline steadily, even as other countries like Japan have raised theirs and gained significant influence by tying aid to a country's purchase of Japanese exports. Our commitments to the World Bank and other multilateral lending institutions have been shrinking, too.

In fact, the entire "International Affairs" portion of the federal budget (which does not include defense expenditures) has fallen by 20 percent in real terms since 1990, and now constitutes merely 1.2 percent of the federal budget. Under such pressures the United States has been busy closing embassies and consulates around the world; nineteen of them were shut during 1995–96 alone, on top of the downsizing of many existing embassies. All this is happening at a time when new political parties and leaders are arising all over the world, when forces hostile to American values are growing, and when the requirements for American engagement are multiplying, and especially in the big emerging markets. "We cannot advance American interests by lowering the American flag," Secretary of State Warren Christopher told Congress. Said Secretary of the Treasury Robert Rubin, "The reductions in funding for the international financial institutions are severely undermining U.S. credibility and leverage throughout the multilateral financial system."

We should not be surprised by such outcomes. Today, no politician gets elected to national office because of his or her "worldview." Domestic issues, narrowly defined, take precedence. Abolish big government. Support or oppose "right to choose." Keep out immigrants. This is a tragic situation for the United States, all the more so because it has become almost impossible to identify world-class statesmen in our legislature anymore. It is legitimate to ask: How will Washington provide the requisite American leadership?

Premature Optimism About America

Although the business expansion in the United States has had a long run, and although both political parties have focused attention on some of the major issues before the country—budget deficits, welfare, health care, crime, and so forth—the fact is that America is badly prepared to meet the economic and social challenges ahead in a changing and brutally competitive world economy. We can do much better, despite the apparent strength of our position today.

Indeed, we should not be complacent, just because the economic statistics of the past few years sound good. Here's why:

- Our projected growth rates are low. From the late 1940s to 1990 the nation's economy expanded on average 3.3 percent per year. In the past six years it has grown at roughly 2 percent. Economists are now projecting a rate of less than 2.5 percent for the next several years.

- Our productivity is declining. From 1946 to 1973 output per American worker rose by an average of 2.7 percent per year. From 1974 to 1995 growth in labor productivity grew at an annual rate of around 1 percent, the second lowest among the top seven industrialized nations.

- Our savings rate is dropping. In the 1970s net national savings was 7.9 percent of GDP, already very low by international standards. In the 1980s it dropped to 4.3 percent. In this decade it has not improved, and is the lowest among the top seven countries.

- Capital investment in recent years has been barely enough to replace old and obsolete plant and equipment. Investment in civilian research and development has remained relatively flat as a proportion of GDP, but since defense-related R&D has been declining, overall R&D has dropped as a percentage of GDP. In fact, since the 1960s, federal nondefense investment as a proportion of GDP has declined every decade for education, R&D, and infrastructure.

- Income inequalities are widening. Pay in the top scales have risen in comparison to those at the lower end of the spectrum. College graduates have gained relative to high school graduates. Older workers have done better than younger ones.

- Incomes have been stagnant for much of the middle class. Until the 1970s, Americans could count on rising incomes—on average, a doubling of income every thirty five years. Over the last twenty years the rate of growth of real wages has dropped in real terms by over 10 percent. Some experts expect that for most American workers real wages will continue to decline for the next decade. In addition, millions of Americans have been the victims of corporate downsizing. Although the economy has generated over 8.5 million net new jobs between 1993 and 1996, the average displaced worker who finds a new job suffered a real wage loss of 10 percent.

• Between 1987 and 1994 a million people a year lost their health coverage, and the total number of uninsured is approaching 40 million Americans, nearly one out of every six.

• The impressive ability of the American economy to generate new jobs masks a growing vulnerability—the growth of the so-called contingent workforce, men and women who take temporary jobs. Some estimates place the size of this group at 30–37 million, about 25 percent of the entire workforce. In an economic downturn these people will be the first to go.

• We've made no provisions to pay future bills. The budget deficit has been declining significantly in recent years, which is good news. But virtually every forecaster says that the decline will soon be reversed if dramatic action is not taken to curtail spending on entitlements. According to current estimates, entitlement benefits in the year 2002 would consume 50 percent of all non-interest expenditures of the federal budget, compared to 40 percent today and 17 percent in 1965. If there are no major changes, by the first quarter of the next century, Social Security and Medicare could lead to tax increases on working people of nearly a third, according to projections by the Congressional Budget Office. As for any significant investment in physical infrastructure, it seems to have fallen off the national agenda.

• The unspoken social contract of the post–World War II era between big American companies and their employees has been torn up. In this implicit arrangement, companies became long-time homes for their workers. The companies trained them, they helped pay for their pensions, and the workers shared their prosperity. For many reasons, including brutal global competition and the ascendance of a type of capitalism that serves only shareholders and not other "stakeholders," this contract has been shredded. There is no set of arrangements to replace it as yet, except a Darwinian free-for-all. That alternative, devoid of mechanisms for training and for maintaining pension and health care benefits while people change jobs, does not constitute national preparedness for the challenges ahead.

- At the same time, the social safety net for the most vulnerable in American society is being removed without adequate planning for transition to another system. The recent dismantling of welfare is a good example. Millions of children will be dropped from the rolls, their parents will be required to work, but the legislation makes virtually no provision for job training and child care. Senator Daniel Patrick Moynihan outlined the implications, calling the 1996 welfare reform bill "the first step in dismantling the social contract that has been in place in the United States since at least the 1930s . . . According to the Urban Institute, 3,500,000 children will be dropped from the rolls in 2001. By 2005, 4,896,000 children will be dropped . . . this bill will cause 2.6 million people to fall below the poverty line."

The combined erosion of both the social contract and the social safety net puts the long-term viability of our economic system in an uncomfortable perspective. Unbridled capitalism in the late nineteenth and early twentieth centuries swung to untenable extremes and produced a populist and ultimately mainstream backlash, which resulted in decades of new regulations for every aspect of the economy—from stock markets to labor practices. It also led to speculative financial bubbles that burst time and again with great damage to the social fabric. The history of other nations was even more violent. England's failure to deal with the social impact of the Industrial Revolution led to over a century of polarization between economic classes. Distorted economic structures in Germany and Japan led to fascism. Historians can argue the particulars, but the main point is that countries that count on the market, and the market alone, to sort out the big political issues inherent in social harmony are taking enormous risks.

Every one of the pressures in our society will get worse if we enter a long recession, a distinct possibility given that the current business expansion is already one of the longest in U.S. history. The combination of competition from abroad and even slower growth would be a double whammy on the most vulnerable portions of the population. With slower economic activity, tax collections would drop and the budget deficit would widen. This could force financial markets to push up interest rates, causing growth to slow further and unemployment to increase. People who would have been on welfare would have nowhere to go but the streets. Our attitudes toward engagement in the global economy, already moving in the wrong direction, could deteriorate even more. Referring to Patrick Buchanan's strident economic nationalism and selective protectionism, Felix Rohatyn, the prominent investment banker and public commentator, was right when he said, "It is frightening to think of the impact of Patrick Buchanan if unemployment were now 7.5 percent instead of 5.5 percent. All that requires is the next recession."

———

Slow growth, low savings, inadequate investment, income inequalities, upcoming budget pressures, and big holes in the social safety net are directly related to the challenge of big emerging markets because they reveal that the American economy will be less equipped to accommodate massive imports, and increasingly vulnerable to foreign competition. They also lay bare a national agenda which will be turning increasingly inward, preempting the time, energy, and resources necessary to address our own competitive position, our need for enhanced access to markets abroad, and the requirement to build better political relationships with the countries that will count the most in shaping the upcoming world order. America, in short, needs a good push to revitalize itself for the era of the big emerging markets.

7 Restructuring Our Policies at Home

Because of our growing trade and financial engagement with the big emerging markets, our approach to economic growth at home is a critical element of an effective strategy for dealing with the Big Ten.

We need to examine all of our domestic economic and social policies for their impact on those segments of the workforce that are already hard hit by stagnating wages, downsizing, and anxiety about job security. Bold departures from current policies will be required.

Even our highly vaunted system of higher education is in need of reform.

ANYONE THINKING ABOUT accepting a position in the government that requires congressional approval must run a gauntlet of senators in advance of the confirmation hearings to exchange views on the job for which you have been nominated. This is a senator's chance to give you a no-holds-barred personal view of what your priorities should be. In my case, these interviews were valuable because they provided a dose of reality that I did not often get once I became the Under Secretary of Commerce. Although I was nominated for a high-level job in trade, what most of the senators wanted to discuss was not our policy toward Japan, the European Union, or China, but the impact of trade on citizens in their home states.

My most memorable discussion was with U.S. Senator Donald Riegle, Jr., Republican from Michigan, who would retire the following year. As chairman of the powerful Senate Banking Committee, he was in a position to block my nomination or to make it sail through. When I went to see him, there were few pleasantries since he wanted to get down to the business at hand. "How often have you ridden in a pickup truck?" he asked. This wasn't my usual mode of travel, so I didn't respond. Besides, I didn't know whether he was serious, for I was expecting a question about the GATT.

He continued, his eyes boring into me. "Have you ever been in a pickup truck after work, and then gone to a bar to have a few beers before going home?" Again I didn't answer. "My guess is," he said, "that someone like you, who has worked almost exclusively in Washington or on Wall Street—we see lots of you guys these days—haven't had this kind of experience. It bothers me a lot. Because it's these guys in the pickup trucks and the bars who are on the receiving end of all the policies you make. Oh, I know that you know the winners, the investment bankers, the top industry executives. But you don't know anyone who is truly struggling to make ends meet every week." And he looked away, and said, "And I wonder how you know what the impact of the policies are on these Americans. How do you know how their lives are affected? Who do you know even to ask?"

Reigle had a point, one which was underscored time and again in interagency discussions over trade policy. Once, amidst a heated discussion of trade strategy toward Japan, I looked around the table and recalled Senator Riegle's question. None of my colleagues would know who to ask.

———

There was a time, when trade didn't mean very much to Americans, when it was most efficient for American trade policy to be made in a compartmentalized way. Some officials would be charged with negotiating market-opening agreements. Others dealt with workers who were displaced because of foreign competition. A third group concerned themselves with foreign policy matters. There was no extensive overlap among the three. As international trade has grown from a small percentage of our economic activity to nearly 25 percent today, it has become a major part of our lives. America's pace of economic growth is highly dependent on trade, and our foreign policy is increasingly concerned with commercial issues. Thus it has become vitally important to deal with all the linkages between trade and other aspects of national policies in a consistent and comprehensive way.

The first Clinton administration made a determined effort to build these connections, but there is still a long way to go. Looking ahead, and anticipating increasing imports from the BEMs, it is important that we do not simply react to dislocations of workers caused by trade, but that we anticipate these dislocations and devise policies that make moving from good job to good job more feasible than it has been. We need to be sure that our economy is as productive and resilient as it can be in order to meet foreign competition head on in the United States and to be competitive in the BEMs, which are already becoming a battleground for American, European, Japanese, and local firms.

As a nation, we face a choice. We can throw up our hands and say it's all too complicated. We can turn our backs on the world and do the absolute minimum that we think we need to do. Or we can identify the most crucial challenges over the horizon, and deal with them with all the strength and creativity that we can muster. This last course would constitute a new notion of national preparedness. It would consist of at least these elements.

We must drop the increasingly artificial distinction between domestic policy and foreign policy. That's the reality in a world where the biggest international challenge we face is in our economic relationships. On the one hand, we will need to pay extra-careful attention to the competitiveness of the American economy. Our workers will need to be able to adapt rapidly to competition from the BEMs. Our companies will need to sharpen their skills in order to compete with their European, Japanese, and local counterparts in the BEMs themselves. On the other hand, our concerns ought to go beyond jobs and profits to our broader role in the world, for it will be on the economic plane that we will succeed or fail in our efforts to influence other countries. If we can work closely with government and business in South Africa or Poland, for example, we will be dealing with the issues that are most important to *their* leaders. As a result, our links to them will become deeper, and our influence will extend to other issues that may become important to us, whether it's mobilizing regional peacekeeping forces in Africa or cleaning up the environment in the former Communist countries.

We must support an exceedingly active role for the United States in the world. The level of engagement required is much greater than that for which our political leaders have prepared us. The sound bites we hear, and which have often become surrogates for foreign policy, such as "We cannot be the world's policeman," are generally couched in the negative. They tell us what we don't want to be, rather than what we need to do. I will address the nature of a more positive notion of global engagement in chapter 8.

We must discard the notion that a "moderate" national agenda will suffice; we need bold policy departures. The conventional political wisdom is that a president has to govern from the center. Perhaps this is true, but it would be unfortunate, to say the least, if such "centrism" is interpreted to mean that we are locked into only incremental changes in the status quo. The essence of leadership is not just to follow what the public wants but to educate American citizens about what they will face if there are not substantial changes in the way we approach the world. To face the coming tidal wave with a philosophy of "steady-as-she-goes" is not to face it at all. Whether we like it or not, the big emerging markets compel us to emerge from our own complacency and to think boldly about what we must do to prosper in the changing global environment.

America's Great Assets

The good news is that America brings enormous assets to these challenges. We are the only real superpower in military and economic terms, and we are the only country in the world willing and capable of being an honest broker in highly charged crisis situations like Bosnia or the Middle East. While we have real economic problems, these pale next to what other industrial nations such as Germany, France, and Japan face. Our industries are rated as being the most competitive, according to authoritative studies done by the World Economic Forum in Switzerland and as evidenced by our phenomenal export performance since 1990. Our entrepreneurial culture remains extremely vibrant—a culture that is tailor-made for an era of new technologies and expanding trade. Our federalist political structure allows us to experiment with many varieties of government-backed economic and social programs; neither Japan nor any country in Europe, with their more centralized government arrangements, can avail itself of such flexibility.

In other words, there is nothing fundamentally wrong with American capitalism. We have the institutions to create enormous wealth, to support our desire for individual freedom, to continue to build a prosperous economy. The big issues do not involve the system itself, but the attitudes and the policies that we Americans bring to the table so that the system works for us amid dramatic changes in the global arena.

We need to use our assets wisely and to put aside the historical cycle of global isolationism and engagement. We cannot afford a tentative approach to global affairs, or any ambiguity at all about sustained involvement. Indeed, the times call for more international activity and engagement, not less. We are increasingly dependent on what happens outside our borders—on energy supplies, on trade, on foreign financial markets—and we have too large a stake in the climate for business around the world not to be heavily involved in the shaping of the global, political, and economic environment. Active American leadership is not a luxury, but our best hope for continued power and influence in the world and for rising living standards at home. After all, if the United States does not provide active leadership, who else will look after our interests? And who will fill the vacuum if we are not in the center of the arena? Who among us would want a world with Germany or Japan or China at the helm? Who would want a world with no one in charge?

What constitutes leadership these days? We know that aiming missiles, moving navies, and sending in the marines has less relevance than a generation ago. We must think about other levers that we can employ.

DOMESTIC POLICY

The OPEC oil embargo of 1973–74 was the first international crisis to reveal how the United States had become interlinked to the rest of the world and how the lines between domestic and foreign policy had become blurred. The imperative was to find ways to use domestic policy to encourage production and energy conservation at home in order to become independent of OPEC. And yet we never achieved that goal; we import a larger percentage of our oil consumption today than we did in 1972.

In the 1980s another linkage arose, as America's position in the world economy changed from that of a net lender to the world's largest debtor; and we became financially dependent on foreign countries who bought U.S. Treasury securities to fund our rising budget and trade deficits. It would have been the right thing to do to reduce our dependence—few experts or government officials would have denied that—but there, too, we did not succeed; today Japan and other foreign investors—governments, institutions, individuals —buy nearly 30 percent of our treasury bonds.

More recently, in 1995 a big debate took place within the Clinton administration over our allegedly dangerous dependence on Japan for technologies for making flat panel display screens, which the Defense Department said were vital for military use. This time, Washington barely tried to achieve independence or self-sufficiency, putting forth a weak program of investment incentives and exclusive government purchasing contracts.

Bottom line: We are not willing to bear the cost to even try to seal ourselves off from international commerce, no matter how much we find it desirable on grounds of national security or sound economic policy. But even if we had the will, such independence from the world economy would be technically impossible, given the tightly woven global economy.

Today the links between domestic and foreign policy are nowhere growing faster than with the big emerging markets, where new competitive pressures will greatly affect the wages and the job security of our workforce. This is all the more serious because these strains will be occurring at the same time that technological change in the United States itself will require even fewer workers to produce a given volume. If the adjustments for our citizens can be made humanely and smoothly, American workers will find new opportunities. The prices of goods and services will be lower, our consumers will be better off. Our growing purchases from our trading partners in the emerging markets will make them more prosperous and give them the capacity to buy more from us. And the chances for political progress in the big emerging markets will improve as economic strains ease. It could be a virtuous circle. But the opposite could be imagined, too—serious problems for American workers, loss of political support in the United States for an open trading system, and growing protectionism, causing a downward economic spiral in big emerging markets because they cannot sell their products and, as a result, less buying from U.S. firms.

Achieving the virtuous circle could happen by Adam Smith's invisible hand. There could be forces in the American economy that create healthy growth and a much fairer distribution of income. The big emerging markets could go through a transitional tunnel of economic and political pain and come out as smoothly operating democracies and free markets. But it is a huge gamble to rely on these trends playing themselves out so happily. In the past, tremendous economic and social change have been far more disruptive. The Industrial Revolution created social tensions between rich and poor within Europe which have lasted to this day. America's own transition to a modern industrial society was tumultuous, with violent labor–management relations, huge protectionist pressures, and financial booms and busts all along the way. Historical analogies should not be carried too far, but surely it is better for America to have a strategy that anticipates the problems that could arise as the world economy undergoes massive structural adjustments and to try to deal with them in as proactive and practical a way as possible.

The Need for Faster Growth

The challenge to the American economy of how to grow faster without igniting inflation is directly relevant to our links with big emerging markets. Since the 1960s, when the economy grew twice as fast as it has in this decade, the average rate of growth has been declining. Not since the Civil War era have we grown so slowly for so long. Such minimal economic expansion aggravates every economic and social problem that America has—from the tensions accompanying stagnant wages of the middle class, to the lack of tax revenue to further narrow the budget deficit, to the pressing need to educate and train a modern workforce, to the need to repair and modernize our schools, bridges, and airports.

Today, most conventional economists believe that the upper limit of healthy growth for the U.S. economy is between 2.2 percent and 2.5 percent. These ceilings seem to be supported by all of official Washington, and Wall Street, too. Experts argue that there is not enough productive capacity in the country—measured by modern machinery, labor, and the productivity of our workers—to produce more without creating inflationary bottlenecks.

But the conventional wisdom assumes we cannot increase productivity even with far-reaching policy changes. By what logic can experts conclude that workers cannot acquire more and better training, or that with an increase in public investment in transportation and education we cannot become even more efficient, or that there are no tax changes, or no amount of deregulation, that can lead to greater savings and investment, knowledge, innovation, and more efficient ways of organizing work? To conclude that nothing substantial can be done to expand productivity, and hence growth, is to say that despite unprecedented changes in technology, dramatically expanding markets abroad, and a new spirit of entrepreneurialism in both the private and public sectors—that despite all this, we're still stuck in a permanent slow-growth rut. It is not a plausible conclusion.

Resigning ourselves to low growth could be a dangerous, self-fulfilling prophecy. Part of the problem is Washington's preoccupation with balancing the budget in so tight a time frame, an obsession that seems to have become the centerpiece for all public policy. This is a recipe not just for domestic retrenchment, but for ignoring the impact on America of new, intense global competition. The reason is that most budget cuts will fall outside of expenditures earmarked for defense, or entitlement programs like Social Security. This means that the burdens of retrenchment will fall almost entirely on what we spend for investment in physical and human infrastructure, from transportation systems to schools. Moreover, the impact of the cuts will fall disproportionately on people most vulnerable to global trade.

It is also unrealistic to believe that the budget can be balanced in so tight a time frame, for there is a strong likelihood that America will see an economic slowdown, if not a recession, well before 2002, given that we have already enjoyed one of the longest periods of business expansion in our history. Under less favorable growth scenarios, tax revenues will decline and deficit reduction targets would have to be revised. Fiscal policy aside, if we remain satisfied with the current level of growth, our companies may succeed in the global arena, but our society will not—not with the prospect of fewer good jobs, not with the wedge that will be driven between the winners and the losers in the economy, and not with the growing focus on domestic problems that will preoccupy Americans at precisely the time we need to be more engaged globally.

Some advocates of faster growth have undoubtedly overstated the possibilities. For example, former vice presidential candidate Jack Kemp proposed an unrealistic doubling of the U.S. growth rate to 5 percent per year. But even a much more modest target would be significant. Today our GDP is about $7 trillion and per capita American income is $26,500. If we grew at 2.5 percent for the next twenty years our GDP would be $8.8 trillion in 2006, and $11.4 trillion in 2016. If instead we grew at 3.5 percent, our GDP would be almost $1 trillion higher in ten years, after inflation, and $2.5 trillion more in twenty years. In real per capita terms, a 2.5-percent growth rate would result in per capita incomes of $30,453 in ten years, $34,950 in twenty years. But 3.5 percent would add an additional $3,150 in ten years, and $7,634 in twenty years. In short, added growth of 1 percent would give Americans much more room to maneuver in a brutally competitive would economy.

THE NEED FOR MORE INVESTMENT

A central issue for the American economy—and for our ability to handle the huge labor adjustments that will be required because of trade with the big emerging markets—is to boost investment. This, in turn, requires increasing domestic savings rates in order to create pools of money from which to draw. There are several ways to do all this, and all need to be part of America's strategic approach to the problem.

While I believe the proposed time frame is too tight, the federal budget must nevertheless move toward balance, so that the government reduces its borrowing in private capital markets and makes way for private business to obtain that money at reasonable interest rates. It is, however, crucial *how* the budget is balanced—whether by retrenchment or by growth.

Balancing the budget in any reasonable period will require a variety of adjustments to existing entitlement programs. All experts agree on the fact that the fiscal burdens of Social Security and Medicare are unsustainable as the population ages and there are fewer younger workers to support them. The system must be fixed. If it isn't, just the cost of four programs—Social Security, Medicare, government pensions, and Medicaid—could exceed anticipated federal revenues. The implication is that there would be a need for massive tax increases, precisely the wrong prescription for an economy that needs to encourage more savings and investment if it is to remain highly competitive in global markets.

Solving the entitlements problem is a herculean task, to be sure, and one hopes that it will be a major focus of President Clinton's efforts in his second term. But whatever the direction that a solution takes, the burden should fall on those most able to bear it, not the middle and lower classes, which are already so buffeted by rapidly changing import patterns. Benefits for the affluent will need to be scaled back with a tax on social security payments to people above certain income levels. The retirement age will have to be raised, so that federal funds will be disbursed over a shorter period of time. In addition, individuals ought to be able to invest at least part of their social security entitlement on their own in 401(k)-type retirement plans. This would help their own retirement, since stock market returns are much more likely to be higher than the very modest annual interest earned on social security funds held by the government. And it would also add hundreds of billions to our capital markets, money that would be available for private sector investments in the economy. Many of these ideas were, in fact, proposed by a Federal Advising Panel at the end of 1996.

The tax code needs to be vastly simplified, as well. The current system is exactly the opposite of what we need. It encourages consumption while inhibiting savings and investment because spending on consumption is largely exempt from taxation while savings are taxed. The consumption bias is reinforced by the fact that the tax code favors debt over equity, by permitting corporations to deduct interest expense incurred by borrowing while taxing retained earnings and dividends; it particularly penalizes long-term equity holding by taxing capital gains attributable solely to inflation. We have been able to get away with this system because of our overwhelming economic strength in the post–World War II era. There is even a strong temptation to think we can still get away with it, given the current troubles of our competitors in Europe and Japan. But this would be a short-term view.

The fact is that over the next few decades, new competitors will be proliferating as will new competitive battlefields here in America and abroad, most acutely in the Big Ten. It is an ill-advised policy to continue to tax our workers and our investors—our human and financial capital—while ignoring other ways to raise revenues. We need a much flatter and simpler tax rate structure with billions of dollars in loopholes closed, but with more IRA-type incentives to save. Fewer loopholes would allow a lowering of tax rates across the board, which would spur people to work and earn more, invest more, and save more. We need to broaden the tax base as well; a national sales tax with rebates for the poor ought to be considered. This would raise hundreds of billions of dollars while putting the onus on taxing consumption rather than investments or savings. Even the unpopular gasoline tax is a good source of revenue; rather than repeal it, as many in Congress have proposed, it should be gradually escalated. We pay by far the lowest price for gasoline in the industrialized world, and the revenues collected could be earmarked for a substantial infrastructure rebuilding effort.

Deregulation must be accelerated. Studies show that in 1995 federal regulations cost the average American household $7,000, whereas the average tax bill was $6,000. As one example, the benefits of airline deregulation have resulted in savings to consumers of over $12 billion annually, according to studies at the Brookings Institution in Washington. Deregulation in the U.S. electrical utility industry—a business larger than automobiles or telecommunications—could save American consumers some $40 billion over the next five years, according to a *Business Week* survey of industry experts. There are a host of issues that ought to be subject to intensive review, with an eye toward further deregulatory action where it is sensible, including environmental regulation, rules for product innovation and safety, and the reduction of the burden of federal paperwork.

Within the constraints of budget balancing, but with a slightly longer time frame within which to do it, more of the nation's public infrastructure needs could be met. The state of our schools and our transportation system, to take two examples, are critical ingredients to enhancing productivity. But the requirements are enormous—$112 billion just to repair secondary schools, $50 billion annually to repair and maintain our highways, $6 billion a year for the airport system. All the more reason for a pro-growth strategy that focuses on raising revenue to balance the budget, and not just on cutbacks in vital expenditures.

INFLATION CAN BE TIGHTLY CONTROLLED

It ought to be possible to maintain the lid on inflation and still adopt the policies outlined above. There already exist powerful anti-inflation forces built into our system as continuous corporate downsizing, weak unions, and substantial foreign competition keep wages from rising. New investment in productivity and heavy deregulation should remove many of the bottlenecks to production that could otherwise cause prices to rise. Imports from the big emerging markets can help, too, for they will create more competition in the United States, leading to more consumer choice and downward pressure on prices. And expanding markets abroad will give us plenty of outlets for our increased production. More growth will mean more tax revenue, which would ease the strain on balancing the budget, freeing up funds for essential public investment—the opposite of the course we are on now.

Besides, there is evidence that concerns over inflation may have gone too far. Important experts, including Federal Reserve chairman Alan Greenspan, have voiced opinions that our methods of measuring prices actually overstate inflation by 1 to 2 percent. This would mean that inflation today is near zero. In the past, many economists once said that there was a natural unemployment rate of about 6 percent, below which prices would begin to shoot up. But during the first Clinton administration, unemployment fell to 5.1 percent with no significant increase in inflation.

A New Social Contract

Faster growth alone is not enough to help the American workforce deal with the problems of adjusting to rapid changes of technology and trade. America must come to grips with the economic insecurity that has become so rampant, a feeling based on wage stagnation and fear of being fired because of corporate downsizing.

These insecurities are directly related to the big emerging markets. The pressures of global competition have suppressed wages and forced companies to cut costs at every turn. We are now faced with the economic and social challenge of needing to be competitive while at the same time ensuring that our workers share in the ultimate success of corporate prosperity. We are a long way from this goal.

As the juxtaposition of strong corporate profits, sky-high compensation for top executives, and stagnant wages for American workers shows, our economic system has swung to extremes in which shareholders and company executives reap virtually all the rewards of increased productivity, and workers almost none. To take a specific case, while productivity has risen at least 1.0 percent each year over the past decade, the average annual gain in workers' real compensation per hour has been 0.5 percent.

Over time this environment will not serve America well. The frustrations of most of our workers will become more acute, not only spilling over into social problems from drugs to crime but also into our competitive position itself, as insecurity undercuts workers' productivity. These same anxieties could lead to growing protectionist pressures.

A new social contract would entail a much closer dialogue between business and labor on the nature of change in the world economy and ways to meet it. It is a dialogue that the government could facilitate, but it would be more effective if top American corporate and labor executives took the lead. There are at least three critical issues: How to share productivity gains with workers in the form of higher wages, how to expand education and training for the workforce, and how to make benefits such as health care and pensions portable from job to job.

The main point is that we are going to have to look at all of our policies through the lens of what they do to workers in the middle and lower income classes, as well as those living in poverty. If we allow the gap between winners and losers to continue to grow, there will be severe consequences to our productivity, our growth, and social harmony. Every major problem we have—from drugs to crime to poor high schools—will be made worse by the workings of the global economy if current trends continue unabated. As a consequence, the BEMs will become huge problems for us, rather than major opportunities.

Rethinking Higher Education

The big emerging markets present a profound challenge for our educational system. There is no need to belabor the improvements that are required in our secondary schools to meet higher standards of math and literacy, since they have been debated at length for several years. Suffice it to say, we need to implement goals that have already been set, and we need to do it on a countrywide basis. National legislation entitled "Goals 2000: Educate America Act" sets forth a respectable plan of educational strategies, including national curriculum standards as well as standards for pupil performance for elementary and secondary schools. In addition, there must be more experimentation with ways to enhance the performance of public schools, such as the establishment of "charter public schools," to be run by a more entrepreneurial cadre of teachers and administrators who are independent of the traditional educational bureaucracy. And yet if this is all we do, we will fall short of what is required for the changing global landscape.

The fact is that even our vaunted university system is in need of change. It is true that we have the best advanced education in the world; witness our ability to attract the more than 450,000 foreign students studying in our universities. But we should not be seduced by our own reviews, for there's a lot more to do. In fact, we give a lot of attention to supplying an American education to foreign students and not enough to teaching our own students about living and operating in a global economy. In the 1994–95 academic year, for example, only 84,000 American students studied abroad, 60 percent of them for just one semester or one summer. The overwhelming number went to Western Europe or Australia. Only two BEMs received more than 1,000 students—China and Mexico.

Much has changed over the last few decades in America's role in the world but, for the most part, higher education has not kept pace. The view from a typical university is that the United States is the center of the world, that our way of thinking and doing things is best, and that everyone else wants to copy us. We have a unique opportunity to do much better.

The study of international relations, for example, will need to take into account the complex interactions between politics and economics since the end of the Cold War. It will require a strong foundation in economics and business, and an understanding of information technology—the forces that now drive so much of the world. But these subjects themselves won't be nearly enough; they will have to be linked to law and politics and culture, just as they are in real life. A powerful emphasis on interdisciplinary teaching will be required, challenging the traditional compartmentalization of academic departments and disciplines. There is no sense in studying the politics of China without having a thorough understanding of China's economic drives and priorities, as well as the historical and cultural setting in which decisions are now being made.

American students will need much more exposure to foreign cultures and languages. This has been the case for years, and meeting the challenge with regard to Europe, with which we share a common heritage, has been hard enough. But because the United States will be so much more involved with Asia, Latin America, and Eastern and Central Europe in the future, the requirements for being able to deal with these societies will be much greater than anything we experienced before.

As more Americans conduct business abroad, they will require more than just an interdisciplinary education, and more than simply a greater sense of foreign cultures. They will need a more acute understanding of how business and government interact abroad—which is very different from the scene in the United States. Such instruction in public–private interaction is rare in our schools, because we start with the assumption that business and government operate in separate arenas.

Americans know very little about the rising generation of leaders in the big emerging markets. There was a time when we could count on U.S. embassies to maintain ties and provide good political intelligence, a time when many of the young leaders wanted to cultivate close links with America. A lot of that was the result of Cold War pressures. A lot had to do with a self-selected foreign elite that defined itself as being connected to America. But in emerging societies today, the key actors are changing fast, and many will have had no contact with the U.S. foreign policy establishment. They will be more preoccupied with taking advantage of revolutionary economic changes in their own countries and with exploiting the world economy for all it is worth. They will be more nationalistic, more riveted on their own societies than on ours. What, after all, do we know about the next generation of leadership in South Africa, a generation which grew up under apartheid? Or about the next generation in Turkey and their feelings about Islam versus the West? Or the ambitions of the future leaders of Brazil, for the first time in a century an emerging superpower in Latin America?

The next generation of leadership in the BEMs are not just "the usual suspects" anymore—not just the government officials or the military leaders—but they are the men and women emerging in the private sector, managers and entrepreneurs. American universities can play a much bigger role in forging ties to these influential men and women by expanding international outreach. This would entail much more than admitting more bright young students into the classroom, but would include mounting special programs in the United States and abroad to involve the up-and-coming movers and shakers. We need to go to them, rather than wait for them to come to us.

AMERICAN BUSINESS SCHOOLS

Given the enhanced role that business will be playing in international affairs in the future, and the particularly crucial role that trade and foreign investment will have on the evolution of the BEMs, the curriculum of American business schools is also relevant to how the United States will meet the challenge of the global marketplace. After one year at the Yale School of Management, I am humbled by the magnitude of the task of educating young men and women in the principles of business and management *and* also inculcating in them a sense of how to do business on a global scale—all in the typical two-year program.

Clearly, however, there are some important principles. All courses ought to be taught in a global context—that is, cases, examples, and research projects should have as a basic assumption that the marketplace is not just the United States but the world.

Students studying economic and political risk should understand the difference between risk assessment in the fifty American states and across national borders. Those studying marketing should understand the difference between promoting a product in Indiana and promoting it in India. The study of leadership should have an appreciation of the different kinds of problems facing a CEO in managing a global enterprise as opposed to a purely national one. Strong courses in business ethics need to come to grips with such critical issues as bribery, treatment of workers, and violations of human rights.

When doing business in the BEMs, future executives will be making decisions in a setting that is constantly unsettled, in which information is never complete, and in which the rules of the game are constantly changing. "Organizations must learn to analyze, adjust, even change direction in midflight, without losing the sense of purpose and action required in the competitive world," wrote Raymond W. Smith, chairman of Bell Atlantic, reflecting on the complex requirements for today's business leaders. Imparting such skills to graduate business students will require new kinds of curricula and new ways of teaching on top of—and not as a substitute for—basic tools and techniques of finance, accounting, marketing, production, and organizational behavior theory.

Future business leaders will also need to be schooled in teamwork to a degree never before envisioned. The complexity of doing business across borders is enormous, requiring teams of product and country specialists. Such teams will have to anticipate and react to rapidly changing situations, putting unusual stress on the group's ability to assimilate information quickly, decide what to do in record time, and work in tandem to do it.

Teamwork among people of the same culture is difficult enough. To do business in the BEMs—to win deals and keep the lead in these hypercompetitive and unstable environments—firms will have to assemble multicultural teams composed of people with different nationalities. By definition, they will not share all the same assumptions or have the same set of experiences or biases. Forging a team based on this kind of diversity will require great skill, and a lot of training.

These considerations raise basic questions not just about the subjects that graduate business schools should teach, but *how* they should teach students who will need to excel in the rough-and-tumble business climates of the BEMs. The methodology of teaching seems to have changed little in the thirty years since I was in college. There may be more information to impart and computers to process that information, but what is called for now is more simulation of real-life situations in which students participate alongside professors and experienced executives. Harvard Business School wisely pioneered the case study, in which students read about a specific business situation and are then grilled on how they would deal with it. The technique could be expanded to live simulated situations in which students and others assume the roles of top executives and board members. The script would call for a case study in which all kinds of unexpected or other special events occur—a currency crisis in a foreign country, a head-to-head competition with another firm which is winning because of a sudden change in its strategy, an opening to win a deal by befriending a government official (with gray-area questions about corruption), and so forth.

American business schools need to move quickly in these kinds of directions. Granted, it is easier to propose solutions than to implement them, in part because there is a lack of professors trained in the techniques of management for a global economy. The fact is that American businesses, not academia, are writing the book on how to do international business, because they are the ones at the frontier of this rapidly changing environment. The times call for more academic research into global topics, more efforts to train professors in this arena, and much tighter links between U.S. business schools and the dynamic firms doing business around the world. These links could comprise more student intern programs, executives who spend time in the graduate programs themselves, and more research on "real-world" situations which students can study.

———

In the 1996 presidential election, President Clinton did not campaign on a platform of bold change. His "bridge to the twenty-first century" is built on a series of small, incremental policy changes—targeted tax breaks for education, small interest-rate subsidies to rebuild schools, the beginnings of a plan to allow workers to transfer their pensions from job to job, small grants to community organizations to help parents to teach their children how to read. While these programs are headed in the right direction, they are far too modest in scope and scale in the context of the challenges we face—challenges that require major changes in growth strategy, in taxes, regulation, portability of benefits, and higher education, not to mention a change in mind-set, to the belief not just that America's competitive challenge is not over, but that it's just begun.

In the 1992 election, Clinton's focus was on strengthening the economy. Four years later, the economy was strong, there was no powerful theme to substitute for it, and so the issues became more scattered. What the 1996 campaign should have been about is a vision of the future—a bold vision, appropriate to the changes that are underway. But although the campaign is over, the United States will be much better off if the big picture is still put front and center, if the issues of growth and social contract are emphasized, and are linked to the broad international challenges. It is not too late, and a young, energetic, and experienced president, one who doesn't have to worry about reelection, could still do it.

8 A Vigorous Commercial Diplomacy

Our foreign policy must shift from a disproportional emphasis on Europe and Japan to paying much more attention to the BEMs.

Commercial diplomacy must become more central to overall foreign policy, more expansive, and more aggressive.

American business also needs an enhanced foreign policy.

IN THE WINTER OF 1994 I was on a trade mission through Latin America. In Brasilia I was briefed by members of our embassy as well as corporate executives from several U.S. companies about a major project in Brazil called SIVAM, a Portuguese acronym standing for "Amazon Surveillance System." The Brazilian government was planning to award a $1.5 billion contract to a foreign company to mount a high-technology surveillance system, using sophisticated radar and satellites over the Amazon Basin. The purpose was to monitor environmental conditions, a task too difficult to fully accomplish in the dense jungle itself. Two consortiums were in a heated contest. One was led by Raytheon, an American firm, the other by Thompson S.A., a state-owned French company. The French government was allegedly supplying extensive financial support to Thompson, and also lobbying hard with Brazilian government officials. Our own government, I was told by American business executives in Brazil, was reviewing the project at low levels in the bureaucracy, with no sense of urgency.

When I returned to Washington, I briefed Secretary Brown as well as key White House officials on the project. We all agreed that because the French government was so active on behalf of its firm, the administration could not afford to be idle. This was especially true because of the nature of the deal in question. The project involved environmental technology, an industry in which the United States was a world leader, and which we had previously identified as a "big emerging sector" with enormous potential for increasing exports. America needed this project not only for the business itself, but because of the precedent; we believed that the new technologies used in this instance would be in demand in other parts of the world, even as far away as Indonesia. In addition, we wanted enhanced commercial links with Brazil, the biggest emerging market in our hemisphere, and we were also conscious that what the United States did there would be noticed all over Latin America. Taking on the French would send a powerful signal that we were serious about commercial engagement in our hemisphere.

A plan was put together under the auspices of the new "economic war room." We decided to mount a full-court press to cut through the usual red tape and to quickly elevate decisions to where they could be made. As step one, Secretary Brown went down to Brazil and lobbied vigorously for the Raytheon consortium. Meanwhile, I pulled together officials from at least ten agencies in Washington to determine the nature of the support we could give to the American firms. The rest of the strategy unfolded quickly. Within days after our war-room taskforce met, the Treasury sent a warning to the French finance ministry that subsidies would trigger a strong U.S. response (which we left unspecified). The administrator of the Environmental Protection Agency sent to her counterpart in Brazil a note indicating that this project was important to EPA, and very subtly implying that future cooperation between the two agencies would be easier if the deal came our way. The director of NASA did the same. The U.S. Export-Import Bank, under the dynamic leadership of Kenneth Brody, promised exceptionally good financing to Raytheon, so that its bidding price could be competitive with Thompson, which itself was receiving extensive financing from the French government. When he returned, Secretary Brown worked the phones to Raytheon and Brazil, seemingly around the clock. Finally, President Clinton contacted the President of Brazil and made his case.

It was a photo finish, but the Raytheon group won the bid.

———

Meeting the challenge of the big emerging markets requires powerful departures from our traditional foreign policy. Of course, we will want to maintain a strong military defense, and, of course, we will have to be vigilant when it comes to protecting ourselves from a resurgence of Russian militarism, or the ascendance of China as a military power. We will want to play a strong role in helping Asian nations to avoid fighting with one another. We should also work to prevent rogue states like Iraq and Iran from acquiring influence. Other areas of traditional foreign policy will remain very important. But equally critical is the need to strengthen the economic and trade component of our foreign policy. We must mount an aggressive commercial diplomacy—far more aggressive than anything we have had to date. And we must rethink the inordinate emphasis that has been placed on close ties with Europe and Japan, and recalibrate the scales so that we devote far more attention to the big emerging markets.

Finance and trade must play a bigger role in our overall foreign policy for several reasons. In the absence of an overwhelming security threat, we can afford to focus on the creation of more and better jobs for our citizens and on raising our standards of living—all of which will result from the establishment of a stable international financial environment and from expanding trade. Moreover, virtually every country in the world is preoccupied with fostering more economic growth, making it more likely that we can find common ground in promoting prosperity. If the United States can engage the big emerging markets on the policies that promote economic progress, our country will make itself more relevant to the Big Ten's highest priorities. As we build the relationships with key leaders across the spectrum of government and business, we will have more influence in noneconomic areas ranging from security policy to human rights—because in emerging markets only a few people are in on the basic decisions influencing the course of their country, and the same few are generally involved across the board.

To the extent that we can have stronger ties with the nations that will be so crucial to the world economy, we will have a better chance to gain maximum benefits from global trade and investment. As a result, we will be a stronger and more confident nation, and more willing to lead in international affairs. No matter what the issue, we would be far less inclined to say, "We can't afford that, because it takes away from what we need to do at home." As a result, we would have more international staying power at a time when more global engagement will be required.

Putting BEMs at the Center of Foreign Policy

We need to do more than rhetorically acknowledge that our policy toward big emerging markets ought to have a stronger commercial dimension; we need to give the BEMs real priority in our overall foreign policy. In what would be a sharp departure from the patterns of the last fifty years, we must reassess where our deepest interests lie over the next several decades, and whether Western Europe and Japan ought to occupy the central places they now do in our thinking, our strategy, and our scarce diplomatic time and resources.

Why this reassessment? First, because it represents the new realities of power and influence in the world. We drew very close to some of our traditional European allies during World War II, and we developed close ties with Japan in its aftermath. Many strong and enduring friendships developed as a result of these experiences. Our economies became intertwined, and we shared a common outlook about political and economic systems. But times are changing.

We must face the fact that Europe and Japan have become our fierce competitors in dealing with the big emerging markets. It would be comforting to think that such rivalries could be benign, but realistically they will not, because they will be about the most central goals of all the countries involved—growth, jobs, and influence around the globe.

At the same time, the course of the European and Japanese economies raises serious issues as to whether they hold sufficient future opportunity for us. Europe has lost much of its technological prowess, its unemployment rate is stuck at a level above 10 percent, and the Europeans are struggling to dismantle enormous social welfare programs in the face of great public resistance. Growth prospects for the next decade are extremely modest, and there is a strong likelihood of economic stagnation and political polarization over economic and social policies. The implications are for a continent that looks increasingly inward, resists further trade liberalization, and shies away from active support of U.S. initiatives—at least those that cost more than rhetorical support.

Similarly, Japan has not emerged as a superpower in any respect. Mired in an economic slump for most of this decade, it remains a relatively closed society, and one that is highly overregulated. Much of its manufacturing sector has moved offshore, and more is in the process of doing so. Trade tensions with the United States have taken a toll on political relations between Tokyo and Washington and on the trust between our respective citizenry. As we get further away from the Cold War, the alliance is weakening, not because of neglect but because of the inevitable rhythms of history and politics.

In the Gulf War, which was the high-water mark of post–Cold War cooperation, Germany and Japan had to be dragged into the coalition against Saddam Hussein. The allies came perilously close to a deep split in their forty-five-year alliance, which might definitely have occurred if the United States had experienced heavy casualties on the battlefield. While the opportunities for close collaboration since then have been less emotionally charged, and the stakes somewhat lower, the record shows that Europe and Japan have not been particularly good allies for America. Up to the Dayton peace accords, there was little cooperation on Bosnia. In America's efforts to stamp out piracy of intellectual property rights in China, Europe and Japan "held our coats, while we went out to do battle," as U.S. Trade Representative Mickey Kantor repeatedly said. When the United States pressured China on human rights, Europe and Japan didn't have time to hold the coats—they were more anxious to take advantage of tensions between Washington and Beijing by presenting themselves as more reliable partners for the big commercial aircraft and telecommunications deals. When the United States tried to isolate Iran and Libya with economic pressure, Europe and Japan thumbed their noses at us and continued to trade.

On more purely economic matters, the prospects for close cooperation between the United States and its traditional allies do not look good. Since the end of the Uruguay Round of trade negotiations, there have been major disputes over trade in automobiles, financial services, and telecommunications. In America's most pressing international financial crisis, the Mexican bailout of 1995, Europe and Japan were essentially absent in the early stages when global financial stability was in jeopardy.

It is not a question of turning away from Europe and Japan; that would be foolish. We will still want to work very closely with these countries, still expand trade, financial, business, and cultural ties. Difficult as it is, we should still try to get their help in all areas of our foreign policy—confronting rogue states like Iraq, fighting against terrorism, stamping out illegal drug traffic, protecting intellectual property rights, and safeguarding human rights. What I propose is a change of the proportion of focus that we give to them relative to the big emerging markets—with a significant shift in favor of the latter.

How would such a strategy operate in practice? It would translate into a strategic plan in Washington that identifies the big emerging markets for more attention, not just as outlets for our exports, but for closer ties in every area that we care about. It would mean refocusing our diplomatic and commercial energies, staffing, and budgets toward China, Brazil, Turkey, ASEAN, and the rest of the Big Ten, such that they were deemed at least as important to us as France or Japan or NATO. It would mean not only reorganizing the entire foreign policy apparatus as it now exists, but changing its European- and Japanese-centered priorities, which are very deeply imbedded in Washington's culture. It would mean giving much more attention not only to economic diplomacy, but to the relation between Washington and American business.

An obvious criticism of this approach is, "How can we get closer to countries whose values are so different from ours, and who are becoming powerful enough to resist all manner of U.S. pressure?" The answer is: It will be very difficult, but that doesn't mean we cannot succeed. Our links with China or Mexico or Poland will never be the same as our ties to England or France, since we do not share the same historical and cultural heritage. We have to think in different ways, not in terms of friends but in terms of interests. And we have to think of ways to satisfy those interests with a new kind of foreign policy. Our time horizon has to be longer than we are used to. Our penchant for making foreign policy through the press, rather than behind the scenes, will have to be reined in because so much of our diplomacy will be dealing with sensitive internal matters in the BEMs—the politics and economics of transition, labor standards, and environmental standards, among other topics. Most of all, we should realize that the crucial playing field is now economic, and that this will require a dramatic new approach to foreign policy.

Commercial Diplomacy Toward the Big Ten

Commercial diplomacy toward the big emerging markets ought to have five priorities. Here's what we must strive to do:

- We must redouble efforts to press for open markets abroad by negotiating additional trade agreements.

- We must build much closer relations with BEMs, including helping them to grow and develop.

- We must help them become more integrated into the world economy, so that they expand the range of their commercial transactions and, at the same time, become more bound by international rules of finance and trade.

- We must expand our economic interaction not just for commercial purposes, but also to gain influence in other arenas, such as human rights and military matters.

- And we must pull out all stops to help our own companies win larger market share in these expanding markets.

None of this will be easy. As emerging markets become more powerful, they will drive much harder bargains. Many of them will become more nationalistic and increasingly disinclined to accept Washington's advice. The bouts of instability in many of these countries will have negative effects on our economic interests and create real problems for us in areas such as human rights. We will, therefore, need a great deal of patience and endurance.

Pressing the Case for Free Trade

The Clinton administration began in 1993 with a crusade to open markets around the world by negotiating a series of new trade agreements. The conclusion of NAFTA, the Uruguay Round, the focus on APEC, and the pressure on Japan were all elements of the strategy, as were the high-profile trade promotion missions of Secretary Brown and other cabinet members. President Clinton captured the essence of his approach in three words, "Compete, don't retreat," and corny as it might have sounded to some people at the time, it was an important phrase.

Unfortunately, election-year politics slowed down the effort, as the administration tried to steer clear of growing concerns about the slowdown of U.S. sales to Mexico and the growing number of layoffs in the United States. It is time now to refire the engines, however, and resume the push for open markets—but this time in conjunction with a deliberate strategy to prepare ourselves for the fierce competition ahead.

There are enormous commercial opportunities for America, opportunities that could generate substantial numbers of high-wage, high-skill jobs. And our firms at this time are in the best shape to compete with their foreign counterparts in over a decade. Moreover, it is futile to resist the change that is coming from new competitors abroad. Protectionism doesn't work in a large, open economy like ours, in which there are already so many links between our industries and those abroad. Our automobile companies, our airlines, our telecommunications firms, our banks are all international now, and a growing number of our most important companies are deriving over half their revenues from overseas operations. Well over a quarter of our trade occurs internally within American firms whose home-based and overseas divisions are doing business with one another across borders. Were we to try to slow this interaction, their businesses would be disrupted severely. Protectionism would also remove the competition which holds down prices and inflation in America. None of these arguments is new. However, under pressure of a changing world economy we need to remind ourselves that the openness of our society is a great strength. But we must also resolve to press other countries in every way we effectively can that they must move toward more openness, too.

GATHERING MORE SUPPORT FROM OTHER COUNTRIES

Commercial diplomacy will require a new style of negotiation. Here, too, it is necessary to expand on the policies that the Clinton administration began during its first term. A good place to begin is to recognize that while America remains the world's most powerful nation, we do not have the clout we once did. We can no longer get our way without mobilizing other countries to help us. The requirement now is to build coalitions of other nations in support of our objectives, not to try to muscle our way alone.

There are several dimensions to improving the way we can operate on this multilateral stage. First, we need to accord more importance to the key global trade institution, the new World Trade Organization. Congress harbors great suspicion about America's surrendering its sovereignty to the WTO, but in the economic realm, where global markets can influence the dollar and American interest rates, or when 30 percent of U.S. growth is reliant on open markets abroad, hang-ups about economic sovereignty are an anachronism. The fact is that the BEMs can be more influenced in the WTO, where multilateral pressure can be brought to bear. It isn't just a question of aggregating the pressure of several countries against one or two of the Big Ten. The more subtle issue is that if members of the WTO press a BEM, it is far easier for the leaders of that country to persuade their domestic constituencies. Suddenly there are "global standards" to meet, "market expectations" to satisfy. Politically, it is a lot easier to accede to those pressures than to the haranguing of Uncle Sam. Admittedly, the United States will not always get its way. We will have to mount an aggressive multilateral diplomacy within the WTO, much as we did in the United Nations on arms control negotiations during the Cold War. This means more time, more effort, and more people who are well trained in the art. If Washington does not take the WTO seriously, it will surely not succeed in achieving its aims. But if it applies all its energy to aggressively courting allies, it stands an excellent chance of attaining its goals a good deal of the time. The WTO is more congenial to our interests than it looks, because the United States had so much to do with writing its rules.

A related aspect of multilateral commercial diplomacy is to encourage the Big Ten to enter a variety of global economic arrangements. This will help bind them to the rules and customs that the United States and Europe have spent decades developing. A good example is Mexico's entrance into NAFTA. In signing the treaty, Mexico obligated itself to a variety of economic policies, including lowering its trade barriers and selling off its state-owned enterprises. The importance of those commitments became evident when Mexico went into deep recession in 1995, and the Mexican government did not abandon its promised reforms. Recently, South Korea joined the OECD. This, too, was an important step in the integration of a BEM into the global economy, for Seoul was forced to take steps and make additional future commitments to open its financial system to foreign investment, among other things. In both cases Washington pushed for the inclusion of BEMs in the broader arrangements, and it was the right thing to do. Elsewhere, Turkey has forged a customs union with the European Union, and Poland is in line for membership in the EU in the future. These are all positive developments.

CHINA AND THE WORLD TRADE ORGANIZATION

Now comes the biggest hurdle of all—whether to allow China to join the WTO. In November 1996 the Clinton administration gave indications that it was reversing its opposition, and was looking for a way to help China gain membership. It would be a good outcome if the two nations could agree on a compromise to make this happen.

In the first place, China's position as a respected member of the global community would be enhanced by its joining the one major organization from which it is now excluded. While its leaders could never admit this publicly, Beijing would benefit by undertaking measures to further open its economy and by being able to point to these international commitments whenever its own domestic protectionist pressures arose.

For the United States the benefits would be large, too. China would be under heavy multilateral pressure to open its markets further. Washington would not have to do all the arm-twisting itself, and could gain help from other WTO members by using the WTO dispute-settlements court. Reducing bilateral trade disputes would give both countries a better chance to build other areas of their relationship. At the same time, however, we have adequate defense mechanisms in our law to prevent Chinese goods coming into our market if they are subsidized or dumped at prices below their production costs; nothing about Chinese membership in the WTO would prevent our using these counter-subsidy or antidumping measures. China's entrance into the WTO would also force it to commit itself to a very specific long-term, timetable for further trade openings—which is a lot more than exists now.

The negotiations will revolve around these issues: What reforms must China take *before* it can join the WTO? And how long should it have to take the remaining steps once it joins? There ought to be a formula that meets requirements for both countries, with China making a substantial "down payment" and given a healthy transition period to implement the balance of the reforms under strict monitoring and supervision, with penalties for failing to deliver on promises. The United States may have to settle for less than all it wants, but the value of having the biggest emerging market in the tent and subject to organized rules and sanctions would be substantial. Indeed, given the importance of China on the world trading scene—not just the size of its market but also its potential to disrupt global business—a WTO without it is not fully functional.

The WTO issue also illustrates the dilemmas of dealing with big emerging markets when there are competing priorities—in this case, trade objectives and human rights goals. Even on strictly commercial grounds the decision of whether or not to admit China is not an easy one, given the trade and investment restrictions that exist in China now. And even in normal times, it would be difficult to totally ignore the human rights situation in China when making major decisions like offering membership into the WTO. But now there is even a bigger problem—how Beijing will deal with Hong Kong as the former colony returns to China's control. If China treats Hong Kong harshly, clamping down on the colony's traditional freedoms, then the chances of its being admitted into the WTO would be dramatically diminished, for it would be too politically difficult for the administration and Congress to move ahead in the face of such provocation.

BUILDING BROADER LINKS WITH INDIVIDUAL BIG EMERGING MARKETS

In fact, greater attention needs to be paid to cultivating our bilateral ties with each of the big emerging markets. A good example to follow is the United States–China Joint Commission on Commerce and Trade (JCCT), a forum that brings top government officials from Washington and Beijing together to discuss ways of cooperating on such matters as trade liberalization, investment disputes, and development of laws for the protection of intellectual property rights. In the first two years of the Clinton administration, the JCCT, which had been established several years before but never utilized except for ceremonial purposes, came alive. In the darker moments of U.S.–China relations, it was an important link among officials of both governments that continued to function when other channels seeemed closed. Between 1993 and 1995, similar forums were established in Brazil, Argentina, and India—in those cases with much more involvement from the business communities of the United States and of the various countries. These kinds of interactions enable each side to raise issues in a nonconfrontational way, and to build relationships among the government and business leaders of the various societies. It may not sound dramatic, but if the effort is sustained and expanded it could over time create networks between the United States and the BEMs that cannot be built any other way, and that can continue to function even during periods when other areas of foreign policy turn sour, as will always happen.

The reason is that in these forums government officials and business executives meet in a unique setting. It is not a negotiation, with all the tension and role playing that that entails. Nor is it a one-shot conference, with all the limitations of a single event. Rather, discussions focus on identifying different solutions to fundamental problems, and the parties know that they will be meeting soon again to examine what progress has been made.

I've sat in on many of these meetings; they are a good combination of substance and relationship building. In the case of Brazil, for example, there have been extensive discussions of how U.S. firms can help to implement the massive Tietê–Paraná River Basin project to clean up one of South America's most important waterways, as well as to enhance the surrounding areas with new transportation systems, industries, and housing. In the case of ASEAN—the forum is called the U.S.–ASEAN Alliance for Mutual Growth—there were efforts to help small American auto parts manufacturers link up with partners in the region.

In the past we have used military-to-military contacts as a vehicle for our foreign policy as large U.S. military assistance missions in which our officers and their foreign counterparts worked together on training, equipment transfers, and even strategic planning. It's a new agenda now, with new players—economic officials and business executives.

EXPANDING TECHNICAL ASSISTANCE

One important part of any bilateral commercial diplomatic agenda will be technical assistance. Considering what big emerging markets will need in order to grow, it is clear that Americans have a great deal of help to provide. We can assist with the establishment of legal frameworks for tax regimes, intellectual property rights, stock market regulation, antibribery legislation, and corporate governance, just to take a few examples. How we accomplish this is a key issue, because our government has few resources at its direct disposal. Cooperative ventures between Washington, the business community, and academia may hold a key. For example, the Department of Commerce works with private attorneys to counsel officials in Eastern Europe on intellectual property rights. During my time in Washington we also began to set up a consortium of American universities to train Chinese professors in all areas of business management so that they could teach Chinese students in such areas as establishing effective corporate boards. These are modest programs, but they point in the right direction. There is a strong case for expanding them.

SPECIAL COMMERCIAL CENTERS

During the time I was at Commerce we established two American commercial centers in the BEMs—one in São Paulo, Brazil, and the other in Jakarta, Indonesia. A third was on the verge of opening in Shanghai. These operations were established outside of the U.S. embassies in order to give them more commercial authenticity. They were designed to help American businesspeople from small and medium-size firms which did not have the budgets or facilities to explore new business possibilities in a foreign country. In these cases, Uncle Sam provided help in the form of temporary offices, showrooms for their products, and counseling concerning how to get information and meet the key people in the country. From the standpoint of American business people, the centers were a marked improvement over what existed before—a few rooms on the second or third floor of an embassy, which could only be reached after having to pass by a marine guard.

These two commercial centers were immediately successful in promoting more engagement between American businesses and their counterparts in the BEMs. It was our plan to establish one commercial center in each of the Big Ten but budget realities have made this unlikely today. This is unfortunate, because for very little investment America could reap not only large returns in terms of sales, but also deeper linkages in the BEMs. If at all possible, more such centers should be built, perhaps cofinanced with export promotion agencies of the fifty states, as well as with rents of commercial tenants.

BROADENING THE RANGE OF CONTACTS

Another aspect of an effective commercial diplomacy involves expansion of the range of people in the BEMs whom we consider to be vital contacts. In the past, American diplomacy was directed almost entirely toward foreign government officials. But in an era where power is becoming more decentralized as a result of deregulation and the growth of private markets, American diplomatic efforts ought also to target governors, mayors, and private business people. We started to do a lot of this in the Commerce Department during my time there. On every trip that either Secretary Brown or I took, we arranged meetings with local officials, the leadership of local chambers of commerce, and students.

One of Brown's important visits occurred when he ventured outside of the city of Bangalore, India, to speak to a group of students about how the world economy was changing for India and America. It was conducted as a classic town meeting, and we were told it was the first of its kind in the country. The Indian media were interested enough to beam the discussion into the homes of 50 million people. In cities like Istanbul, Turkey, or Cordoba, Argentina, I spent many hours talking to mayors and local business leaders about developing deeper links with American companies. We were clearly just scratching the surface, and much more official involvement outside of the capitals is required.

MORE VIGOROUS AND FOCUSED TRADE PROMOTION

In the time I was in Washington, the term "commercial diplomacy" had different meanings to different people. To most of the executive branch it translated as "export promotion." To the Republicans in Congress, export promotion translated as "corporate welfare"—government subsidies to companies—and the Republican congress elected in 1994 tried to eliminate it.

Neither view was the right one. Export promotion is a very important part of commercial diplomacy, but it was still just one part. And it would be a dangerously shortsighted move if Congress were to eliminate or eviscerate these programs. Certainly they can be made more effective—which programs cannot?—but the federal government has been successful in helping thousands of firms, big and small, win contracts in situations where they otherwise might not have prevailed. These cases are documented in reports to Congress concerning the National Export Strategy that make reference to what companies themselves say.

Besides, total funding for U.S. export promotion has been declining in recent years. In 1994, the federal government spent approximately $4.5 billion to help American exporters, but by 1997 the amount was closer to $2.8 billion, a drop of nearly 40 percent. Much of this decrease took place in promotion of agricultural sales, but every program is under great pressure.

Compare this to America's competitors. When I was in the administration we regularly surveyed our embassies in Europe and Japan to get a better understanding of how other countries were promoting their exports. All our main competitors devoted more money and more staff to export promotion than we did relative to their GDP. In 1995, France spent ten times as much as the United States did on export promotion staff (relative to GDP). In 1996 Ottawa outspent Washington by a factor of ten when it came to trade shows, trade missions, and other nonfinancial export promotion (again, relative to GDP). In 1994, Japan provided ten times the absolute amount in financial assistance to its exporters that America did (in part as a result of foreign aid available for export promotion).

Along with a relentless focus on efficiency, the government ought to be expanding these programs if we are serious about achieving vital goals at home and abroad. And, given the scarcity of resources, more ought to be focused on the BEMs. Not only are these the markets of the future, but they are the ones where governments have thrown up the most obstacles to U.S. sales, and the ones most unfamiliar to American businesses. The Commerce Department has in fact made dramatic reallocations of funds to programs in the Big Ten, but more could be done by other agencies.

There also ought to be more targeted efforts to help small and medium-size business—the most dynamic part of our economy—to export. The objective should not be to create a new committee in Washington or to hire a few additional civil servants, but to re-examine how to encourage the American banking system to provide more extensive financing for overseas expansion of small firms.

Moreover, the entire federal export apparatus, strewn as it is among several agencies, ought to be consolidated into one power-house of an agency. There would be substantial efficiencies in such a merger, which could bring under one roof the U.S. Commercial Service, the Export-Import Bank, and the Overseas Private Investment Corporation (which provides insurance against expropriation and other political risks). American firms would appreciate such one-stop financing in place of the complicated mosaic that now exists.

WINNING COMMERCIAL CONTRACTS—
ENHANCING THE "ECONOMIC WAR ROOM"

A particularly crucial aspect of an export promotion strategy is to step up the federal government's role in helping U.S. firms to win contracts in the big emerging markets. Of course, companies must first ask for help, but if they do, and if they meet the set of legal and ethical guidelines that the administration has issued, they should get it, particularly if the deals will result in the creation of good jobs in the United States. The rationale for this government role is that it will be a long time—if ever—before the commercial environment in the markets of the Big Ten is as free of government interference, overt or in the back rooms as it is, say, in England. The fact is that in all the BEMs, governments are the entities that are awarding contracts and they are influenced by the interest shown by other governments. If Washington doesn't show up in support of our firms, it's a sure bet that Bonn or Tokyo will do so on behalf of theirs, putting our companies at a major disadvantage.

Before 1993 the United States was not well prepared to help its firms in the brutal global competition to win large-scale projects. True, Washington had helped companies in the past—the Bush administration had assisted AT&T in winning a large contract in Indonesia, for example—but these were ad hoc efforts, usually at the eleventh hour. Early in its first term, the Clinton administration decided that a far more systematic strategy was required, one that would make use of all the diverse resources of the federal government. The new approach anticipated upcoming commercial contests in which American firms needed help, so that the proper groundwork could be laid. In many big emerging markets, however, even after contracts are signed there can be a host of problems before the shovel ever enters the ground; therefore, effective U.S. help had to continue well beyond the initial stages of the deal. The new strategy therefore tried to build links between a group of people in the government and the American firms bidding on projects, so that Washington could interact with companies, first to gauge whether a project was, in fact, in the public interest, then to help win the deal. Then to make sure it went forward. This, in turn, required assembling a group of professionals who could understand all aspects of the project, including the industry and the particular economic and political considerations in a specific foreign country, as well as the conformity of the project to U.S. law.

And so the "economic war room" was established as a center for

policy, information, strategy, and follow-through, and as a government nerve center for coordinating the efforts of a host of government agencies. It began to coordinate everything from lobbying other
governments, to behind-the-scenes advice to U.S. companies, to government-backed financing. It helped the administration systematically think through the criteria for helping U.S. firms, criteria that
revolved around perceptible benefits to the U.S. economy, including
support of the jobs at home that would result from increased exports.

The importance of the war room goes well beyond the billions
of dollars in contracts it helped American firms win. The effort
symbolized the importance of commercial priorities in American
foreign policy. It conveyed to our competitors and to the BEMs that
we were deadly serious about expanding our commercial reach in
big emerging markets, and that involvement of U.S. firms in building the infrastructure in a foreign country was a key element in
America's links to the most dynamic areas of the world. It was also
an unabashed acknowledgment that the commercial playing field
in the world economy is not close to being level, and that other
governments—Bonn, Paris, Tokyo, Ottawa—have been backing
their firms for years.

In Washington there is a chronic disease that makes officials
think that if there is a new initiative, and if the press writes about
it, then it's time to move on to something else. When it comes to
the war room, that would be a big mistake. The center is in its in-
fancy and in a tenuous state now that the initial publicity is over.
This is an institution that needs to be nurtured and expanded. It
needs the support of the highest administrative officials. It needs
to be staffed by specially recruited men and women with requisite
project-related skills. It's a sure bet that other governments will
not let up on their efforts to help their firms, because such assistance is embedded in their culture. We let down our guard at our
own peril.

Some have criticized this effort to help U.S. firms win contracts
on the grounds that it runs contrary to free-market philosophy. But

the fact is that there is no other way to open markets without significant pressure. Moreover, other governments are providing help to their firms in a major way, and have been doing so for years. Should we sit back and let them win the contracts, gaining the jobs and the profits and also building the all-important formative commercial relationships?

A more recent criticism is that in picking executives to go on high-profile trade missions, or in identifying projects that the government should promote abroad, the Clinton administration played favorites and rewarded major campaign contributors.

In my time at Commerce, the trade missions contained a wide variety of participants. Some were prominent business leaders who were Democrats, but there were many long-standing Republicans, too, and several who hedged their bets by contributing to both parties. Our principal concern was not the executives' party affiliation, but the extent of their involvement in the countries to which we were traveling, so that we could highlight their projects to the foreign leaders who had the clout to help close the deals. We also wanted businessmen and women whose firms were prepared to break into new markets and could take advantage of the pressure that Secretary Brown exerted on overseas leaders. And there were other factors as well: making sure that each delegation contained some representatives from small and medium sized firms, and also from minority-owned companies. Anyone looking through the lists of executives who went on these trips would see that the composition nearly always conformed to these criteria.

When it came to the war room, we would swing into action on behalf of a company only after it had completed a legal and ethical questionnaire that had to pass the muster of government attorneys. This information was also reviewed by our embassies abroad to make sure that we had obtained as much background as possible on the company, its activities, and the project in question. Once that happened, there were two major issues left. First, we had to satisfy ourselves that there was a rationale for any government involvement at all. This usually boiled down to making sure that the deal in question was being influenced elsewhere by some other national government, and therefore required Uncle Sam's help to level the playing field. Second, our primary criteria for helping a company was whether we could demonstrate that jobs would be created in the United States as a result.

If the Congress or the administration moves to reform these procedures, they must be sure to do so without crippling our ability to compete in a decidedly imperfect world. By all means, we should have better rules and reasonable disclosure where it does not now exist. But it would be suicide to tie ourselves in legal knots, as we Americans are so often prone to do, when every other major government is expanding its support for its firms without putting itself in a straitjacket that subjects every detail to public debate, and eventually becomes so constricting that it is impossible to act at all. What is at stake here is not just the interests of a few companies, but jobs, economic growth, political influence abroad—all that our total foreign policy should be about these days. The public and private sectors have no choice but to work together if our nation is to derive the full set of benefits of a changing world economy. How we do this must always be under serious review. But challenging that basic premise of partnership would reveal a profound lack of understanding about the world that is emerging.

REORGANIZING THE FOREIGN POLICY APPARATUS

It will be impossible to implement a vigorous commercial diplomacy unless the entire foreign policy bureaucracy is reshaped for a new world in which economic engagement with the big emerging markets is the centerpiece of our foreign policy. This is a major task, and few steps have been taken so far. There are huge obstacles, including the preponderance of State Department officials who are trained in political and military affairs, as opposed to commercial matters; the fundamental bias to favor traditional allies like Great Britain and traditional military hot spots like the Middle East in all areas of our diplomatic efforts; and the overall budgetary constraints as the entire diplomatic corps undergoes a major downsizing. Still, the reengineering must be done. During the first Clinton administration, our embassy in Brazil had only 6 American commercial officers, while there were 42 Americans assigned to political and military issues. In India the ratio was 6 to 52. In China it was 13 commercial officers to 38 political and military. In Poland 3 to 28. Resources devoted to the analysis of economic trends and policies were widely skewed toward Europe and Japan, even though that kind of information is widely available in the private sector. For example, Japan had 22 economic analysts, compared to 12 for India and 11 for Brazil.

A foreign service that has a much higher proportion of professionals who understand economic and commercial diplomacy would require recruiting men and women with a variety of skills and backgrounds that are underrepresented today in the State Department, or even in the Commerce Department. These include men and women with advanced degrees in economics, business, and technology. Recruiting at the mid-career level, where significant real-world experience can be found, must also be vastly expanded.

A foreign service and a broader civil service organized in this way would allow Washington to implement and sustain a more aggressive commercial diplomacy, rather than just articulate it. It would give successive administrations the ability to build stronger ties to the Big Ten, preoccupied as they are with economic and commercial issues, and in the process would facilitate American objectives of broader access for U.S. firms. It would put the United States in a much stronger competitive position vis-à-vis Europe and Japan in the increasingly intense trade battles for market share in the BEMs.

COMMERCIAL DIPLOMACY AND HUMAN RIGHTS

One of the great dilemmas in advocating an aggressive commercial diplomacy is that it may appear to assign a higher priority to international trade than to American values. In numerous debates within the Clinton administration and in Congress, there has been heated discussion over whether we should continue normal trade with China despite its record of human rights abuses. We face this dilemma, as well, in those countries that do not treat workers fairly, or those that fail to take environmental protection seriously enough.

I firmly believe we should stand up for our principles, and that we should be as persuasive as we can with foreign governments whose regimes fail to measure up to our standards. But we must be clear-eyed about the world that is evolving, and about the best strategy to achieve the results we want. Such a strategy, whether it concerns labor rights, broader human rights, or environmental protection, ought to be based on several principles.

We should use political pressure, when necessary, but adopt a bias for behind-the-scenes diplomacy rather than policy-by-megaphone. When we have sensitive issues with Germany or Japan, we try to deal with them outside of the glare of the media. It is the best way to avoid a strong nationalistic reaction. If we treat the BEMs differently, then we are misreading their significance and risking making the problems worse.

We should look for multiple opportunities to highlight standards for labor practices, human rights, environmental protection without tying standards to trade itself. There are several possibilities. We should, for example, redouble efforts in the International Labor Organization or in the U.N. Human Rights Commission to improve the conditions for people everywhere. Multilateral pressure can be applied when one of the BEMs is applying for membership in one or another heretofore "exclusive" club—the OECD, NAFTA, ASEAN, the WTO (in the case of China). A good example is South Korea's entrance in the fall of 1996 into the OECD. As part of the price of membership, Seoul had to reform its existing labor laws in order to bring them into line with the standards of the International Labor Organization's charter. This required the repeal of arrangements relating to labor–management relations left over from the military dictatorships of past years. The OECD will now monitor carefully the implementation of Korea's commitments. In January 1997, in fact, the OECD censured Seoul for violating its agreements, thereby putting significant international pressure on the government to get back into compliance. This is a much different kind of pressure than directly linking trade concessions to human rights. It is saying to a BEM: "Our group stands for certain standards relating to civil society. You need to meet them if you want to sign up and remain a member in good standing."

Washington should also lend its encouragement to private efforts to focus on abusive human conditions. It should publicly applaud efforts like the one made in November 1996 by the Federation of Sporting Goods Industries, whose members include Nike, Reebok, and Adidas, which set a deadline of February 1997 to end the abuse of child labor in Asian nations, It should support organizations that attach labels saying where products originate and the conditions under which they are produced, thereby giving consumers as much information as possible to factor in their own values when making purchases. Washington could also confer public distinction on firms that adhere to the highest moral standards, and it could encourage American business leaders to do the same in their various trade associations.

But tying labor standards, broader human rights, and environmental issues to trade would be self-defeating unless many other countries joined us—which, if history is a guide, will be almost never. The reason that we cannot succeed alone is that the U.S. monopoly on virtually any product has disappeared; whatever we withhold, some other country is likely to supply. And because of pressure from American business, the United States has not shown great staying power when it comes to unilateral sanctions. We thus get the worst of all worlds—political tensions, lost commercial contracts, and, eventually, a reputation for being an unreliable supplier, thereby further jeopardizing our commercial interests for the longer term.

We should adopt a mind-set that trade is an asset to enhance the values we hold dear, not a liability. There are prominent commentators on the left and the right who allege that trade shores up repressive regimes, and that we should withdraw trade privileges in countries like China or Indonesia. The counter-argument is much stronger—provided it is properly articulated. That argument is that over time, economic progress loosens political control over people's lives. We have and will continue to see this happen all over the world. In the democratization of South Korea, Taiwan, Argentina, Brazil, Mexico, and Poland—to name a few—the economic genie is out of the bottle, and the people of those countries are beginning to hold their governments more responsible for increasing economic and political freedoms. The more trade, the more growth. The more growth, the greater popular expectation that there will be more opportunity for better jobs and a higher standard of living. In today's world economy, countries can achieve this goal only with substantial links to global markets, which means increasingly open societies. Granted, China and Indonesia are two BEMs which have thus far been able to retain tight political controls. Not everyone moves at the same pace. But for them, too, change is coming, peacefully or violently—but it is coming.

With economic and political liberalization will come better living conditions, unless the BEMs are totally immune from the patterns of history. It would be overstating the case to say that trade is the total answer to America's quest for higher standards—far from it. But it certainly can play a positive role.

We should seek nonpolitical ways to enhance our values abroad. Our foundations, think tanks, and universities can also play an important role in furthering human rights by providing technical assistance for developing the institutions that safeguard rights in any society—whether that means training judges and lawyers, educating civil servants, or fostering links through influential academics with ties to governments abroad. All this will help lay the enduring foundations of more just societies among the Big Ten. But we must remember that these nations are too big, complex, and nationalistic to be changed or swayed by U.S. arm-twisting. Only change that comes from within the countries themselves will work, and that means the development of the rule of law, and regulations and the capacity to implement such law rigorously, consistently, and fairly.

In sum, we should not let up on our human rights activity, even as we divorce it from trade policy.

Secretary Brown set a good example on a visit to Beijing in 1994. Brown was scheduled to see the President of China, Jiang Zemin, for a half hour. Instead, the meeting lasted about 90 minutes. Brown started by pressing hard for China to approve two big contracts, one for Chrysler and the other for McDonnell-Douglas. Then he turned to human rights. He was an old civil rights lawyer, he told Jiang, and he, as much as anyone, knew that the United States still had big human rights problems. He admitted that he was in no position to preach to China, but the fact was that China's hopes to be a big and respected power were being hurt by the way political dissidents were treated. Brown reeled off several names of people he had in mind. He was not going to say anything publicly, he said, but countries with good relations—as he hoped the United States and China would have—needed to deal with one another frankly in private.

The President of China paused for a long time. "I can deal with you," he said, "because you didn't come here pointing a finger in our face." And then he went on to discuss the human rights picture in China, how he saw it, how others saw it. And he agreed to reopen a formal discussion between the two governments, a discussion which had been halted several months before. Then Brown went back to the Chrysler and McDonnell-Douglas deals, making the case that these were good deals for both countries.

This story illustrates several dimensions of commercial diplomacy—including why its importance extends beyond business transactions. Brown would never have had the audience if he had come solely to talk about human rights. But he had an attentive head of state a few feet away because in the potential auto and aircraft transactions lay the future of China's economy. Brown practiced commercial diplomacy, in the broadest sense—using economic engagement to further a whole set of U.S. goals beyond simply the business contracts at hand.

This approach to human rights is an unsentimental policy prescription. It is a call for realism over idealism, but for a means to achieve our idealistic goals over time. The pace of liberalization and development in the big emerging markets is unprecedented. The winds are with them and us. Within a decade, if *economic* progress continues, we will be living in a world much more congenial to our values.

A Strategy for American Business

It is easy to think of American companies as bestriding the globe. After all, long before the term "multinational corporation" became a buzzword, firms like Ford, IBM, or Coca-Cola were household words in countless nations. Today, Levi Strauss, Xerox, and McDonald's are seemingly everywhere. And new names like Microsoft and Starbucks are popping up, too.

But as international as we think our companies are, for the most part, they have been focused on Europe. Total business across the Atlantic—which includes both trade and foreign investment both ways—is twice the amount of cross-Pacific commerce. Japan has been the second most important focus for American firms, but breaking into that market has been notoriously difficult, and generally only the biggest firms able to spend millions in development costs have succeeded in building major businesses. In the Big Ten, American firms have a long journey to travel. The fact that companies like Citibank, General Electric, or AT&T are devoting so much of their efforts to entering emerging markets should not be confused with their achieving scale in these countries. Most of them have a toehold compared to what could be possible. The hundreds of thousands of medium-size and small American companies—the ones that don't make the top lists of *Fortune* and *Forbes* but that create most jobs in America—are barely in the game.

It is critical for America that our firms establish themselves in the BEMs. Enhanced American sales abroad mean better jobs at home. Studies by the Commerce Department and the National Association of Manufacturers show, for example, that export-related jobs generally pay 15 percent more than the average manufacturing wage, and tend to be much less vulnerable to economic downsizing or to economic cycles in the United States. American firms operating on a global scale will also have opportunities to play on a larger and more diversified field, which means higher earnings, more opportunity to finance the escalating costs of research, and more ability to weather the ups and downs of any one market.

From a national standpoint, the enhanced involvement of U.S. firms will spread American influence around the world. Companies like Johnson & Johnson or Gillette are building ties with hundreds of millions of consumers in Mexico, Brazil, India, Indonesia, and China. IBM and Microsoft will build links to most everyone who turns on a computer. Boeing and Bechtel will train and build bridges to thousands of engineers in emerging markets. This influence is crucial because it is aimed at the areas with which people in emerging markets are most concerned: better jobs and higher standards of living. It is influence which becomes all the more important as our military presence abroad, so long an emblem of American strength, gradually recedes.

The involvement of U.S. companies in the BEMs will make an enormous difference in how the Big Ten enter the world economy, and the time frame in which it happens. If you hang around Washington long enough, it could appear that the World Bank or the

International Monetary Fund or U.S. trade negotiators are the driving force for integrating emerging markets in world trade and finance. The truth is that a far more important factor are the business deals struck between foreign and local firms. International companies provide money, technology, management, and distribution channels to local entities—and this is where the rubber really meets the road.

American firms will also be a primary medium for the transmission of our values. Companies like Procter & Gamble are setting the standards for health and safety in their plants in India. Levi Strauss is funding antidiscrimination groups in Brazil and has made racial diversity an explicit goal of hiring there, breaking new ground in Brazilian culture. American International Group is providing extensive training opportunities for its employees in China—many more than they could ever get from Chinese companies. WalMart, the Gap, and Disney have stepped up efforts to monitor their many subcontractors all over Asia and Latin America to ensure that wages and treatment of workers are fair. This isn't to say that much more shouldn't or cannot be done—but these and many other companies are moving in the right direction.

The next few years provide an especially important window of opportunity for American companies to press for more access to emerging markets. The momentum of economic openings in these countries is strong. U.S. companies have rarely been so competitive. The Clinton administration has demonstrated a willingness to systematically help American firms break into foreign markets and conclude deals, and, if it has the will and the foresight, it could do even more.

These next few years are critical, as well, because this is the time when formative relationships will be made between U.S. companies and local business leaders and government officials who are gaining influence during the dramatic transitions that so many big emerging economies are undergoing. The old cast of characters is being shaken up, and it will pay huge dividends to build ties with the emerging leaders.

When I was in the Clinton administration, my colleagues and I received a vivid demonstration of the importance of a firm's being in on the ground floor. The case in question was a competition between several U.S. firms and Siemens Corporation of Germany to build the subway system in Guangzhou. It was to be the first modern subway in China, which was planning to build many more for its enormous cities. Siemens won the contest, we believed, because it received significant financial support from Bonn. But the importance of the victory extended well beyond the deal, because Siemens then had the inside track with key people who would make decisions on the other mass-transit systems. The Germans would have the only major demonstration project to showcase in China. They would have met the crucial decision makers in China's State Planning Commission, which has so much to say about major infrastructure projects, as well as the transportation authorities. And they would have had unprecedented experience in adapting their product to Chinese requirements. Such is the value of seizing the moment.

THE NEED FOR AN EMERGING-MARKET BUSINESS STRATEGY

American firms need to rethink their business strategies in light of the difference between the environment in big emerging markets and the more mature and predictable markets of Europe. There are several imperatives.

Doing well in a big emerging market requires a long-term horizon. If companies are not willing to place long-term bets, they shouldn't be in the game. But there is slight paradox here, too, because at the same time that they look well into the future, companies will need to be adaptable to changes in the short term. Our firms will need to brace themselves for ups and downs of governments, economic policies, and huge demographic changes. They will need to refine their ability to assess risks, but without knowing all they want to know—all they might search for in mature economies—

because no sooner would they gather such information than it would be outdated. Consequently, there is a great premium on extreme flexibility—in corporate structures and in strategic thinking.

American companies increasingly will have to move from exporting to manufacturing in the big emerging markets themselves. This is what their competitors will do to get closer to consumers, to raise funds on local markets, and to tap into the local talent. They will also have to be prepared to share some technology with local firms, or else they will find themselves losing big contracts to their competitors.

U.S. firms will need to devote more attention to recruitment and training of staff that can operate in different cultures. This has always been a challenge in global business generally, but the emerging markets present an even more daunting task. In my discussions with top American CEOs, a current refrain is the need to "globalize the management culture." It has been easier to find a person to head up an operation in Brazil or China, where a capable native manager is found, than to develop in the corporate headquarters a top management team that can operate across borders and cultures. Yet this is where U.S. firms need to be headed if they are to take full advantage of the enormous commercial opportunities in a dynamic world economy.

American companies will have to learn to manage a difficult balance: how to build a multinational workforce and still maintain a clear corporate identity and corporate values. It will be a serious challenge for companies employing men and women from Mexico, Poland, Turkey, and South Korea to maintain a global strategy and a global set of ethical principles while vigorously pursuing local business in countries of such diverse history, politics, culture, and business climate. But without a strong corporate identity, transmitted and understood by all of a company's managers and workers no matter where they are, the top executives will lose all control of strategy and standards. Not only will they not be able to compete effectively because they cannot coordinate their cross-border operations, but they will be mired in a host of problems that their American boards and constituencies will object to—from corruption to unfair labor practices. A minimum requirement will be for extensive training of staff around the world with regard to corporate strategy, corporate culture, and corporate standards.

A FOREIGN POLICY FOR AMERICAN BUSINESS

Most companies think about foreign policy as something that Washington alone conducts. Most corporate public affairs departments or government relations offices are typically focused on Washington, not Warsaw or Seoul. In the Big Ten, however, every firm will have to know how to deal with the central government authorities. American companies are going to need their own foreign policy.

A business foreign policy not only would aim at understanding and influencing the way Washington works; it would devote even more time to figuring out how foreign governments in the big emerging markets are likely to behave. We live in an era where new faces are appearing all the time, where policies are in flux, where huge economic and political pressures are converging on governments that are ill equipped to manage a free market system. It is thus imperative that a large number of American firms—not just a handful of big oil companies and other multinational companies—understand foreign politics and the way they could affect business prospects and decisions.

Another area of business foreign policy would concern the involvement of a firm in the local society. For many decades American multinationals—mostly big mining and energy concerns—were the whipping boys for criticism that American firms take from foreign countries and return very little except money. They subvert the culture and the environment, so the argument went, while maintaining oppressive working conditions for local labor. These arguments are not heard so much any more, not just because the BEMs are so keen to attract more foreign investment, but also because U.S.

firms have become much more sensitive when operating abroad. However, they face even larger challenges in the future, especially in the Big Ten.

Many of the BEMs, like South Korea and the ASEAN nations, have themselves become much more sophisticated about what they expect from multinational corporations—more and better jobs, improved working conditions, and technology. They are driving much harder bargains, and they are playing one firm off against another to squeeze out the best commitments. But American firms also have an interest in creating an environment in which they are welcomed and considered part of the local community. They need the markets more than ever. They must rely on a loyal and trained local workforce. And in a world so closely tied by communications, they do not want the adverse publicity at home of having treated local communities in, say, India with less consideration than they would treat workers in the United States. At home *and* abroad, American firms will have to answer to society's demands with respect to ethics, the environment, jobs, diversity, and social responsibility.

The amount of work that firms will have to do to become an accepted part of the local scene in emerging markets will increase dramatically. Local populations themselves are becoming much more aware of their own leverage. Also working against foreign firms is the growing uncertainty and anxiety among local groups in emerging markets, for as governments recede, and private economic activity expands, there will be a vacuum of order, a new level of chaos, in which foreign firms are blamed for all the problems that occur during times of tumultuous transition.

American firms will have to be on guard for shifting political winds which can derail major investments. A classic recent case was the Dabhol power project in India, a $2.8 billion investment in the state of Maharashtra by a U.S. consortium led by Enron, and including General Electric and Bechtel. In 1994, Enron received permission from both national and local authorities to go ahead with this project, the largest foreign investment ever mounted in India.

When a new government was elected in Maharashtra in mid-1995, however, the contract with Enron was summarily canceled, even though construction had begun. The newly elected governor accused Enron of negotiating a "sweetheart deal," since Enron had won its contract without competitive bidding. According to the same politicians, Enron had been allowed to charge electricity prices that were too high, leading to electricity bills for Indian citizens that would be unnecessarily expensive. Enron was also accused of winning by bribery—a charge vigorously denied by the company, never substantiated by the Indian authorities, and eventually dropped.

There ensued six months of high-stakes drama. Enron was forced to shut down operations. It spent $250,000 per day just to keep the plant in condition to reopen. Passions in India rose against the allegedly exploitative foreign company. Enron started legal proceedings. Behind the scene the American ambassador tried to restart negotiations. Other American companies, fearful of a deteriorating investment climate, threatened to pull out.

Eventually, Enron and the government of Maharashtra agreed to renegotiate the original deal. After winning some twenty lawsuits and spending several million dollars, a settlement was announced in December 1996, and the project was allowed to proceeed.

But the broader lesson is applicable to other U.S. investors, and reflects key principles: In big emerging markets, it pays to anticipate rapid changes in the political climate, and to go to great lengths to cultivate ties with opposition candidates and with every element of the surrounding community. It pays to have backing from the American government, but especially to have a savvy ambassador who is skilled at commercial diplomacy, someone who understands the art of calming tempers rather than inflaming them, and the virtue of operating behind the scenes rather than through the public media. It pays to be totally clean with regard to bribery; this is, in any event the right thing to do, but also in this particular case, had there been any evidence that Enron had made payoffs, it would have emerged under the glare of so much international attention that the deal could never have been put back on track. And finally, it pays to go through a process of open, competitive, transparent bidding—even when the awarding government does not demand it. In that way there can be no questions of exploitation or favoritism. All these issues reveal the complex and highly volatile environment in which U.S. firms have to operate in emerging markets.

The case of Coca-Cola in China likewise illustrates the complexity of doing business in the BEMs, even for one of the world's largest and most powerful companies. Coke formed an alliance with the government of China in which it traded access to the market for technical assistance on plant hygiene, packaging, and distribution as well as assistance to farmers to start a new line of fruit drinks. Coke has brought in prominent entrepreneurs from Hong Kong as partners in China. It has invested millions to adapt its marketing and advertising to a Chinese audience. It is training its Chinese employees in the basics of finance, labor relations, and other management skills—up to 1,800 students in 1996. Even after all this, there was no certainty about Coke's future. In May 1996, for example, the Chinese government gave signals that it would curb Coke's expansion to protect local soft drink companies. While it appears that Coke will get what it needs, clearly there are obstacles all along the way.

Another aspect of a foreign policy for American business is closer cooperation with other American firms abroad. The local American chambers of commerce and the various industry associations face a major challenge. The Japanese and European business communities in the BEMs are typically much more tightly woven than their American counterparts. They have their own information-gathering operations, their own trade-promotion efforts, their own training facilities to educate foreign workers. American companies will have to combine forces in a similar manner if they are to maximize their considerable influence. In the past U.S. firms relied heavily on Washington for information and for leverage. They will have to do much more themselves now, because the federal government's resources—and skills—are often inadequate.

Once, on a trip I took to Indonesia, the top executives of one of the American auto companies brought up an interesting problem. They were thinking about expanding their operations, and were pointing out that to do so they would have to depend on Japanese companies in Indonesia for automotive parts. For competitive reasons, it made them uneasy to buy from, say, Toyota, because the suppliers would have an important window on the American companies' entire operation. They explained how companies like Toyota encouraged their parts manufacturers to come to Indonesia to serve Toyota, and even helped them set up shop. Then they painted the broader picture in which Korean and Taiwanese companies in other industries were also encouraging their parts producers to join them, establishing special industrial parks so they could all be close together, pool costs, and cooperate on design and inventory management. I asked the American company whether they contemplated doing the same thing—that is, asking an American supplier to join them. "No," they said, "but that's a good thing for you in the Commerce Department to do." I politely told them they'd be waiting a long time, because if it was in their interest, it was for them to do it.

American companies also need to educate boards of directors in the realities of doing business abroad. Each of the issues discussed here—economic opportunities, political and economic uncertainties and risks, corruption, human rights, environmental protection, need for long-term horizons, and extreme flexibility in planning and operations—requires corporate directors with a level of experience not often found. As U.S. firms expand abroad, the qualifications for corporate governance will need to change, with understanding of global realities given much more priority. Sophistication over and above what would be necessary to deal with European-type issues will be particularly required to oversee business strategies and standards in the Big Ten.

The Need for Public Awareness

For most of the Cold War era, educating the American public about the realities of international life was relatively easy. There were allies and there were enemies. There were competing ideologies. A huge amount of public discussion revolved around the adequacy of national defense. American firms were strutting around the globe, and only in the last several years, with the rise of Japan, did competition begin to appear worrisome. As citizens, we needed to know less about the global environment, so it seemed, to understand what was happening to our own lives and why. And we trusted our government to give us most of the information that was needed.

So much has now changed. International affairs have become more complex, and with the emergence of so many new powerful countries on the scene, that complexity is going to keep increasing. At the same time, there has been an explosion in the availability of up-to-date information by the media and the Internet. There's more to understand, and the information is coming at us from every direction.

When it comes to America's changing role in the world, however, the public is not getting the information it needs. Coverage of international issues is declining as Americans care less about global issues than about their own neighborhoods, and few in the press are trying to make the crucial connection between the two. In 1985, for example, 24 percent of the articles in *Time* and 22 percent in *Newsweek* were devoted to international news, but in 1995 the percentages were 14 and 12, respectively. "There is a diminution of coverage," said Mortimer B. Zuckerman, chairman and editor-in-chief of *U.S. News & World Report*, "simply because they are less relevant." He's wrong about the relevance, but the fact remains that this is how many executives in the media see things.

Understanding that the rise of big emerging markets represents the central strategic challenge of our times requires helping Americans to understand that these new power centers present great opportunities and great risks. Americans need to know more about both. But it's not just the press that's deficient; we need to hear more from Washington, more from our business leaders, and more from the educational establishment.

The importance of public awareness in a democracy like ours is obvious, but it cannot be overstated. For one thing, a new kind of framework for America's role in the world could not possibly be supported and sustained if American citizens do not understand what's changing and why. They have to have a clear idea of the stakes involved in the big emerging markets, the ups and downs which will characterize our relations with them, and the reasons for those ups and downs. They need to see the links between our interests abroad and our policies at home—what we have to do to be even more competitive than we are, while addressing head on the problems of workers who will be hurt by rapidly increasing imports. Without some public consensus on these issues, our policies will swing from pole to pole, guaranteeing a rudderless approach to a challenge that cries out for a consistent, long-term view.

———

Combined with a domestic strategy that recognizes the need for a proactive approach to the new world we are entering, a vigorous commercial diplomacy will help the United States to remain a powerful and prosperous nation. The risk is less that our leaders will disagree with the prescription outlined above than that they will not be aggressive enough in implementing it. It all depends on whether the revolution in economics and politics wrought by the big emerging markets is recognized for what it is, or whether we all get distracted by the events of the day. I remain optimistic that we will rise to the occasion, because we always have. But there's an awful lot to do in the next several years if our faith in America is to be justified by the reality.

9 | America's Choice

IN THE SUMMER OF 1993, after President Clinton indicated his intention to nominate me to be an Under Secretary of Commerce, but before I officially began work at the department, I met with some friends with whom I had worked during the Carter years to get some advice on how to prepare for my new job. It was a good group to talk to, because they had become prominent Washington lawyers, and had kept up their involvement at both ends of Pennsylvania Avenue. I, on the other hand, had been living in New York, Tokyo, and Hong Kong as an investment banker since my previous stint in government in the mid to late 1970s, and I was out of touch with the scene in the nation's capital.

I asked the group some broad questions about whether government had changed, what they viewed as the most pressing policy areas, who was up and who was down. A variety of advice was dispensed, some good, some off-the-wall, but one comment remained in my mind throughout my government service: "You had better arrive knowing precisely what you want to accomplish," one person said, "because once you begin work, the press of events and demands will be so great that you will be prisoner to your 'in box' and to outside events unless you have your own objectives and are determined to achieve them." I remember an analogy another person used: "You will be on a luge," he said, referring to the sled that moves faster and faster in a steeply inclined circle, in which the drivers seem unable to do much but hold on and try not to fall off.

Looking back now, I'd like to think that Secretary Brown and I had a vigorous proactive plan, and that we tried to orient American thinking and action in a clear direction. The plan, of course, focused on the big emerging markets and closer engagement with them. Needless to say, we didn't discover the BEMs; many innovative companies had already geared their strategies toward them. And President Clinton's foreign policy inevitably had to come to grips with the complex issues of China, Mexico, India, Indonesia, and many more of the Big Ten. But we did try to give some coherence to the concept of big emerging markets, to break new ground when it came to helping to expand America's commercial reach abroad, and to nudge along others in the administration to think more comprehensively about the implications of a BEM strategy for the longer term.

As I have said, the Clinton administration was quick to embrace the concept, but only the first steps have been taken so far, and there is a lot more to do. At issue is not just a vigorous approach to promoting America's exports abroad—although I think we can do even much better than we have, and we must—but also broader engagement with the Big Ten in helping them to make the transition to democracy and capitalism. There are great opportunities for the United States, because the BEMs are the new economic frontier, with their enormous craving for all kinds of consumer goods and their requirements to build everything from airports to health care systems. But there are major uncertainties and risks, too, for there is no assurance at all that the big emerging markets will "emerge" in the way that Americans would like, that they will be economically and politically stable, that they will not become nationalistic power centers challenging or opposing us in various parts of the world or in important international organizations.

In fact, only a super-idealist would say that America is not going to have big troubles with the BEMs. All the other countries that burst on the world scene in the last century—Germany, Japan, Russia, even the United States—have brought turmoil in their wake, politically, economically, socially. The rise of the BEMs today is no different—they are redefining political power in the world and re-shaping the global economy. The issue is not whether the United States is in for a very rocky period of international affairs, but how we handle it. Will we recognize the nature of the challenge? Will we understand the requirement for approaches radically different from those we followed in our foreign relations before? Will we see the BEMs as a challenge that blurs the old distinctions between foreign and domestic affairs and requires the ultimate fusion of the two? Will we think differently about the requirements for leadership in business and education, and relate them to the BEMs? These are the big questions.

America has risen to the occasion before in this century: briefly in World War I, more fully in World War II, and in the Cold War. This time, however, the challenge is more difficult.

We face a period of great uncertainty for a long time, because the outcome of the political and economic transitions in the Big Ten will not be clear until well into the next century. Indeed, our traditional goal of seeking a "stable" world must give way to something much more ambiguous. There will be no stability for a long time.

We no longer have a common enemy to unite us as a nation. Moreover, rather than facing war or the threat of it—also a force for unity—our big challenges relate to commerce or values like human rights, which can be internally divisive.

We cannot fall back on our history, because a radically new world with new pressures and new leaders requires new guideposts for navigation. The targets for our international diplomacy are not just other sovereign governments, as has been the case for so long. Our diplomacy will involve regional entities like ASEAN, and also the private sectors of the BEMs, where so much of the critical activity will take place.

We face excruciating dilemmas in balancing trade, security, and human rights concerns in the BEMs, but our objective should be to maintain some consistency toward the goal of closer engagement with the Big Ten.

We will need our traditional allies, but we will also be competing fiercely with them for the markets we all desperately need. Lacking a common military enemy, these rivalries will surely change our relationships much more dramatically than diplomats are now willing to admit.

We must learn to think about national policy in new ways, not just in terms of what Washington can do but what our business and educational sectors can contribute.

And we face a huge hurdle in conducting a national dialogue on all these complex issues at the very time when the public is hooked on sound bites and the media is feeding the habit.

In order to rise to *this* occasion, the United States must not be the hapless driver on the luge, taking the turns as they come, reacting rather than leading. We must resist falling back only on what we have known, and recognize the revolutionary nature of the times. We need to rid ourselves of the smug feeling that because we are such a powerful nation, and because our economy is riding high, then all the other potential problems are minor. We need a clearer definition of our purpose and our goals.

In the end it would be misleading to think that we can shape events absolutely to our liking. We cannot control the global flow of goods and money. We cannot control technology. We cannot control the human passions of billions of people who, for the first time in our memories, believe they can have a much better life, and wanting it *now*.

What happens in the Big Ten is mostly up to them. But we shouldn't underestimate the extent of our influence if it is wielded consistently, if we make the effort to build coalitions of other countries to support our goals, and if we deal sensitively with the internal pressures operating within each of the big emerging markets.

———

As 1996 ended, the newspapers were again reflecting on the kinds of interaction America will have with the BEMs. President Clinton was signaling that in a second term he would go to China to put our relations with Beijing on a stronger footing. A big Indonesian conglomerate was accused of trying to influence American policy through campaign contributions, kicking off a major scandal and a renewed focus on campaign financing. NATO seemed ready to admit Poland into the alliance. Washington was frustrated with South Korea for failing to open its market to American companies, even as that nation experienced the most extensive labor demonstrations in its history. The administration was angry with Turkey for cultivating ties with Iran, and with South Africa for flirting with arms sales to Syria—both in defiance of expressed American desires to abstain. Financial markets were anxious about the course of economic policy in Mexico, Brazil, Argentina, South Africa, and India. It was a complicated mosaic which could be interpreted one of two ways—either as the normal ebb and flow of world events, or as the uneven but inexorable movement of a new category of country to the forefront of the global stage. You decide.

The German statesman Otto von Bismarck said, "World history, with its great transformation, does not come upon us with the even speed of a railway train. No, it moves in spurts but then with irresistible force." So it is with the rise of the big emerging markets. Over the next decade there will be fantastic opportunities in this great transformation for America. There will be enormous pressures and risks, as well. We can play the new global game without a bold strategy, hoping for the best with marginal adjustments to what we are already doing, or we can adjust to the changes with all the energy we can muster. It's a choice that America will make, even by default. But in reality, what choice do we have?

Appendix

Snapshots of the Big Ten

Plus the Chinese Economic Area, ASEAN, and Mercosur

For sources and other explanations, please see key on page 214.

THE BIG TEN

MEXICO

BRAZIL

BOLIVIA
PARAGUAY

"Mercosur"
Argentina
Bolivia
Brazil
Chile
Paraguay
Uruguay

CHILE

URUGUAY

ARGENTINA

POLAND

TURKEY

CHINA

SOUTH KOREA

HONG KONG

INDIA

TAIWAN

VIETNAM

"Chinese Economic Area"
China
Taiwan
Hong Kong

MALAYSIA

BRUNEI

PHILIPPINES

SINGAPORE

"ASEAN"
Brunei
Indonesia
Malaysia
Philippines
Singapore
Thailand
Vietnam

INDONESIA

SOUTH AFRICA

Argentina

Population	34 million
Land Mass	1,170,622 square miles (four times the size of Texas)
Capital City	Buenos Aires
Language	Spanish
Form of Government	Federal republic; bicameral legislature and president elected every four years
UN Development Ranking	30th
Freedom House status	Political rights = 2; Civil liberties = 3
Communications	1 telephone per 7 people; 1 television per 4.6 people
Average GDP per capita, 1991–1995	$7,307.40
Average annual GDP growth, 1991–1995	5.3%
Average unemployment rate, 1991–1995	10.2%
Major Industries	Food processing, flour milling, chemicals, autos
Major Imports	Capital goods, passenger vehicles, petroleum products
Major Exports	Meat, wheat, corn, manufactured products

U.S. Merchandise Imports from and Merchandise Exports to Argentina

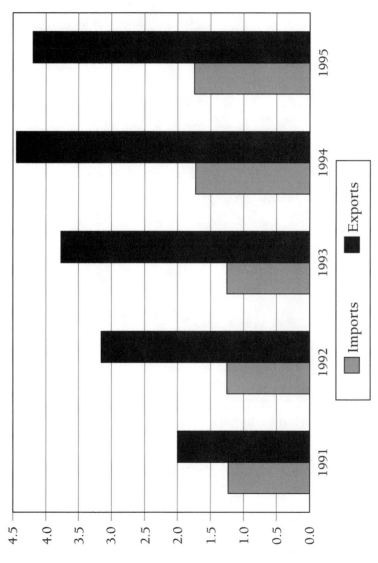

Brazil

Population	160 million
Land Mass	3,511,965 square miles (slightly smaller than the continental U.S.)
Capital City	Brasilia
Language	Portuguese
Form of Government	Federal republic; bicameral legislature and presidential elections every four years
UN Development Ranking	58th
Freedom House status	Political rights = 2; Civil liberties = 4
Communications	1 telephone per 10 people; 1 television per 5 people
Average GDP per capita, 1991–1995	$3,233.00
Average annual GDP growth, 1991–1995	2.7%
Average unemployment rate, 1991–1995	5.1%
Major Products	Steel, autos, metallic minerals, coffee, sugarcane, soya
Major Imports	Machines/electrical materials, crude oil, chemical products, grains, coal
Major Exports	Iron ore, soybean bran, orange juice, footwear, coffee, auto parts

U.S. Merchandise Imports from and Merchandise Exports to Brazil

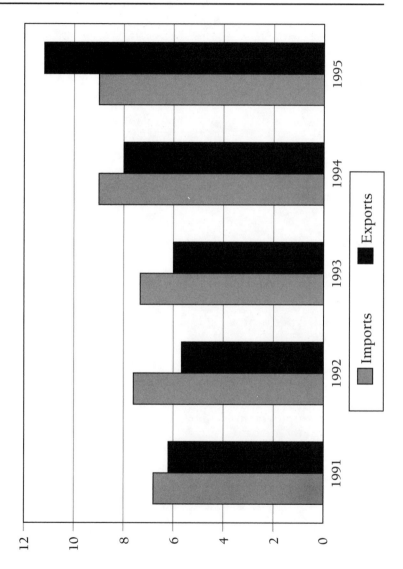

China

Population	1.2 billion
Land Mass	3,696,100 square miles (slightly larger than the U.S.)
Capital City	Beijing
Languages	Chinese/Mandarin, Cantonese, Shanghainese, Fuzhou, Hokkein-Taiwanese, Xiang, Gan, Hakka dialects, minority languages
Form of Government	One-party rule
UN Devevelopment Ranking	108th
Freedom House status	Political rights = 7, Civil liberties = 7
Communications	1 telephone for 77 people; 1 television for 32 people
Average GDP per capita, 1991–1995	$424.20
Average annual GDP growth, 1991–1995	11.1%
Average unemployment rate, 1991–1995	2.6%
Major Products	Iron and steel, coal, machines, armaments, textiles and apparel, rice, potatoes, peanuts, tea, pork, cotton, fish
Major Imports	Rolled steel, motor vehicles, textile machinery, oil products, aircraft
Major Exports	Textiles, garments, footwear, machinery and equipment, weapons systems

U.S. Merchandise Imports from and Merchandise Exports to China

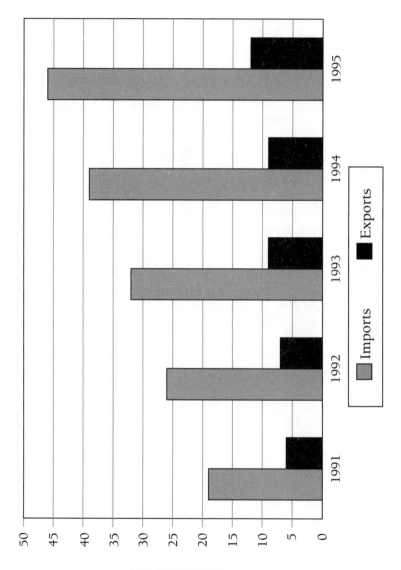

India

Population	937 million
Land Mass	1,222,559 square miles (one-third the size of the U.S.)
Capital City	New Delhi
Languages	Official language is Hindi with English as associate official; 24 languages spoken by a million or more people
Form of Government	Federal republic
UN Development Ranking	135th (lowest of the Big Emerging Markets)
Freedom House status	Political rights = 4; Civil liberties = 4
Communications	1 telephone per 145 people; 1 television per 44 people
Average GDP per capita, 1991–1995	$310.40
Average annual GDP growth, 1991–1995	4.7%
Average unemployment rate, 1991–1995	N/A
Major Products	Steel, autos, metallic minerals, coffee, sugarcane, soya
Major Imports	Capital goods, petroleum products, chemicals, pharmaceuticals, fertilizers
Major Exports	Clothing, gems and jewelry, chemicals, leather, engineering goods, fabric, cotton yarn

U.S. Merchandise Imports from and Merchandise Exports to India

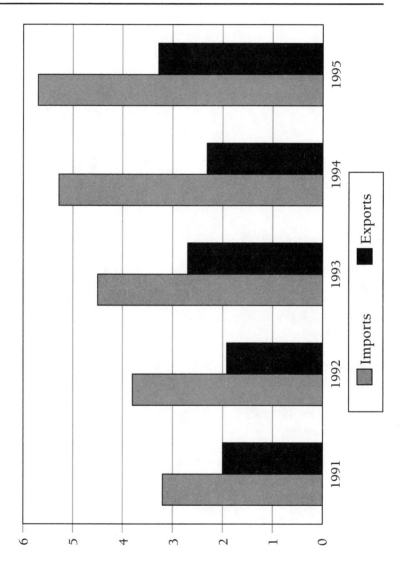

Indonesia

Population	203.5 million
Land Mass	741,052 square miles (slightly less than three times Texas)
Capital City	Jakarta
Languages	Malay (official), English, Dutch, Javanese
Form of Government	Strong presidential republic
UN Development Ranking	102nd
Freedom House status	Political Rights = 7; Civil Liberties = 6
Communications	1 telephone per 122 people; 1 television per 17 people
Average GDP per capita, 1991–1995	$839.40
Average annual GDP growth, 1991–1995	7.7%
Average unemployment rate, 1991–1995	2.47%
Major Industries	Food processing, textiles, cement, light industry
Major Imports	Machinery/equipment, chemicals, fuels, raw materials
Major Exports	Crude oil, oil products, plywood, natural gas, garments, textiles, rubber

U.S. Merchandise Imports from and Merchandise Exports to Indonesia

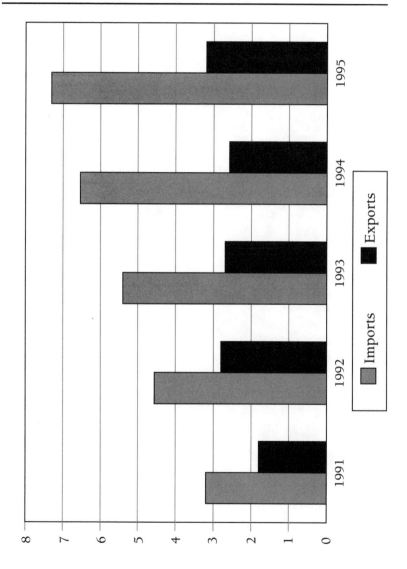

in billions US$

Mexico

Population	94 million
Land Mass	756,066 square miles (almost three times the size of Texas)
Capital City	Mexico City
Language	Spanish
Form of Government	Presidential federal republic; single-party rule for past fifty years
UN Development Ranking	48th
Freedom House status	Political rights = 4; Civil liberties = 4
Communications	1 telephone per 8 people; 1 television per 6.7 people
Average GDP per capita, 1991–1995	$3,507.80
Average annual GDP growth, 1991–1995	0.8%
Average unemployment rate, 1991–1995	3.8%
Major Products	Food/beverages, chemicals, iron and steel, petroleum, mining, textiles, clothing, vehicles, tourism
Major Imports	Metal-working machines, steel mill products, agricultural machinery, electrical equipment
Major Exports	Crude oil, oil products, coffee, silver, motor vehicles, engines, cotton, electronics

U.S. Merchandise Imports from and Merchandise Exports to Mexico

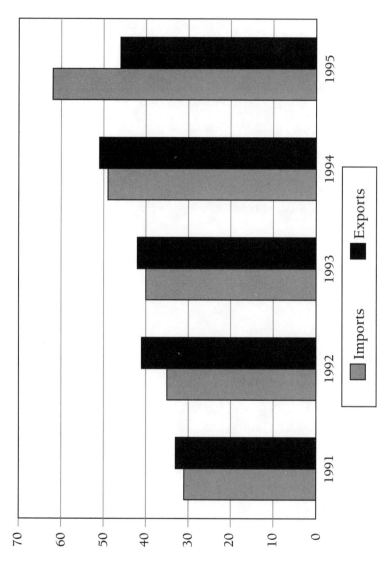

Poland

Population	38 million
Land Mass	120,727 square miles (slightly smaller than New Mexico)
Capital City	Warsaw
Language	Polish
Form of Government	Presidential/parliamentary republic
UN Development Ranking	56th
Freedom House status	Political rights = 2; Civil liberties = 2
Communications	1 telephone per 7 people; 1 television per 3.8 people
Average GDP per capita, 1991–1995	$2,378.20
Average annual GDP growth, 1991–1995	2.32%
Average unemployment rate, 1991–1995	12.78%
Major Products	Shipbuilding, chemicals, metals, autos, food processing, grain, potatoes, sugar beets
Major Imports	Machinery and equipment, chemicals, food, light industry
Major Exports	Machinery and transport equipment, foodstuffs, manufactured goods

U.S. Merchandise Imports from and Merchandise Exports to Poland

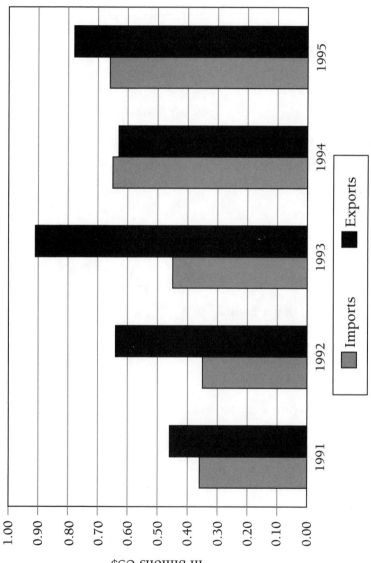

South Africa

Population	45 million
Land Mass	473,290 square miles (almost twice the size of Texas)
Capital City	Pretoria
Languages	Eleven official, including Afrikaans, English, Ndebele, Pedi, Sotho, Swazi, Tsonga, Tswana, Venda, Xhosa, Zulu
Form of Government	Federal state with nine provinces; president elected by National Assembly
UN Development Ranking	100th
Freedom House status	Political rights = 1; Civil liberties = 2
Communications	1 telephone per 7.5 people; 1 television per 11 people
Average GDP per capita, 1991–1995	$3,050.60
Average annual GDP growth, 1991–1995	0.8%
Average unemployment rate, 1991–1995	45% (more than 50% in some homelands)
Major Products	Gold, platinum, chromium, steel, tires, auto assembly, textiles, metalworking, dairy products, poultry, wool
Major Imports	Machinery, transport equipment, chemicals, oil, scientific instruments
Major Exports	Gold, minerals and metals, food, chemicals

U.S. Merchandise Imports from and
Merchandise Exports to South Africa

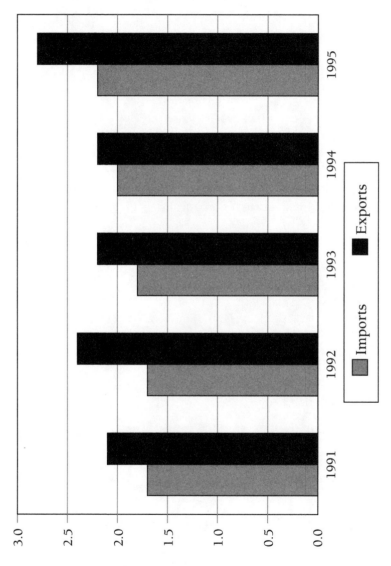

South Korea

Population	46 million
Land Mass	38,330 square miles (slightly larger than Indiana)
Capital City	Seoul
Language	Korean
Form of Government	Presidential system
UN Development Ranking	29th
Freedom House status	Political rights = 2; Civil liberties = 2
Communications	1 telephone per 2.5 people; 1 television per 5 people
Average GDP per capita, 1991–1995	$7,801.60
Average annual GDP growth, 1991–1995	7.5%
Average unemployment rate, 1991–1995	2.48%
Major Industries	Electronics, ships, textiles, clothing, rice, barley, autos
Major Imports	Machinery, transport equipment, fuels, chemicals, grains
Major Exports	Electronic and electrical equipment, machinery, steel, autos, ships, textiles

U.S. Merchandise Imports from and Merchandise Exports to South Korea

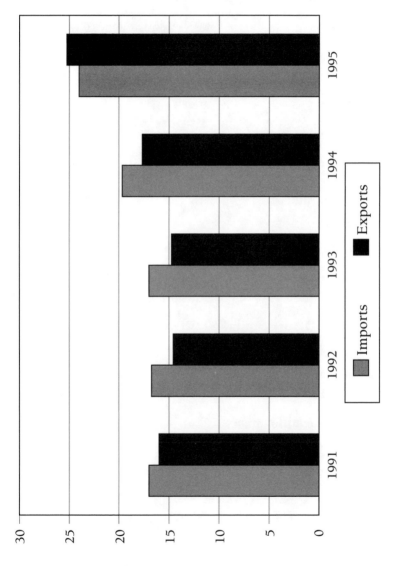

Turkey

Population	63.5 million
Land Mass	300,948 square miles (twice as big as California)
Capital City	Ankara
Language	Turkish
Form of Government	Parliamentary republic with prime minister; president elected by General Assembly every seven years
UN Development Ranking	84th
Freedom House status	Political rights = 5; Civil liberties = 5
Communications	1 telephone per 5.7 people; 1 television per 5.6 people
Average GDP per capita, 1991–1995	$2,628.60
Average annual GDP growth, 1991–1995	3.3%
Average unemployment rate, 1991–1995	7.8%
Major Products	Iron, steel, machinery, cars, tobacco, cereals, cottons, barley
Major Imports	Petroleum, chemicals, textiles, machinery, vehicles, iron
Major Exports	Manufactured products, foodstuffs, mining products

U.S. Merchandise Imports from and Merchandise Exports to Turkey

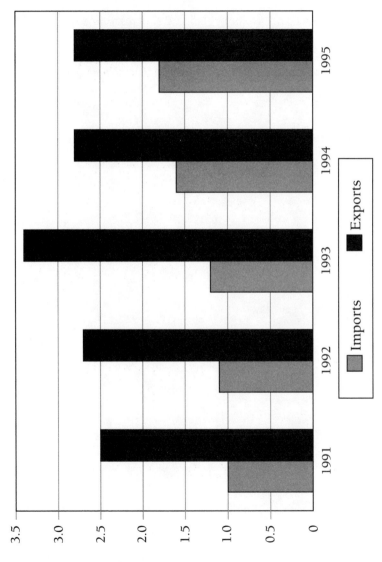

ASEAN (Association of Southeastern Asian Nations)

Combined Population	425 million
Combined Land Mass	1,537,228 square miles (slightly smaller than a third the size of China)
Capital Cities	Bander Seri Begawan, Jakarta, Kuala Lumpur, Manila, Singapore, Bangkok, Hanoi
Members	Brunei, Indonesia, Malaysia, the Philippines, Singapore, Thailand, Vietnam

U.S. Merchandise Imports from and Merchandise Exports to ASEAN

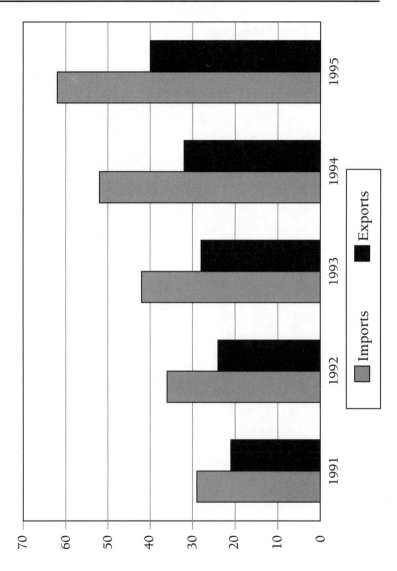

Chinese Economic Area

Combined Population   1.23 billion

Combined Land Mass   3,709,940 square miles (slightly larger than the U.S.)

Capital Cities   Beijing, Victoria, Taipei

Members   China, Hong Kong, Taiwan

U.S. Merchandise Imports from and
Merchandise Exports to the Chinese Economic Area

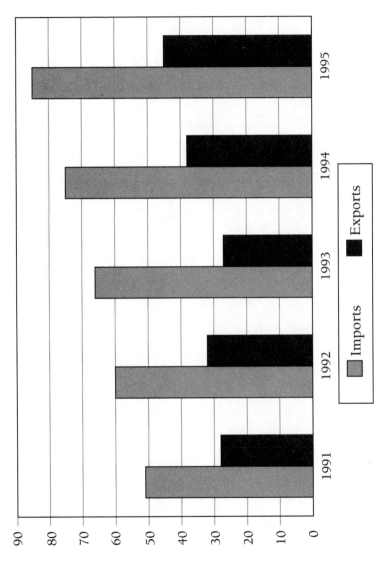

Mercosur

Combined Population	198 million
Combined Land Mass	4,585,073 square miles (larger than Canada)
Capital Cities	Buenos Aires, La Paz, Brasilia, Santiago, Asunción, Montevideo
Members	Argentina, Bolivia, Brazil, Chile, Paraguay, Uruguay

U.S. Merchandise Imports from and Merchandise Exports to Mercosur

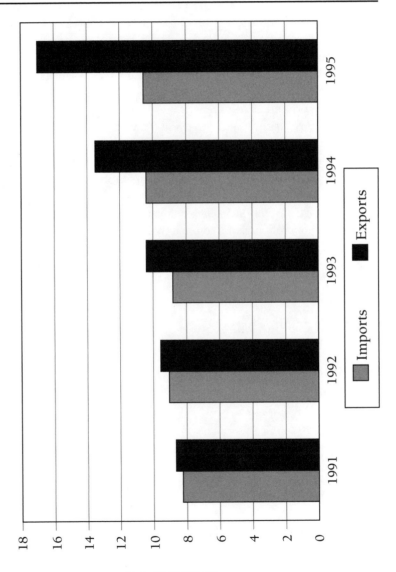

Sources

NONSTATISTICAL COUNTRY DATA

The World Factbook 1996–1997, published by the Central Intelligence Agency, information provided to them by a number of sources

Country Reports from *The Economist* Intelligence Unit, various annual and quarterly reports, 1994–1996

The World Almanac, published by Funk & Wagnall's; Robert Famighetti, editor

Reuters, daily on-line news reports

The United Nations Human Development Index, which is calculated by the United Nations Development Program. Ranking is out of 174 possible countries and based upon statistical measures of life expectancy, educational attainment, and adjusted per capita real income. Available in various United Nations Development Program reports

Freedom in the World 1995–1996, published by Freedom House, a New York–based nonprofit organization that monitors political rights and civil liberties around the world. The categories of political rights and civil liberties range in a scale of 1 to 7, with 1 being the most free and 7 being the least.

STATISTICAL COUNTRY DATA

Country Reports from *The Economist* Intelligence Unit, various annual and quarterly reports, 1994–1996

Country Reports from The Institute of International Finance, Inc., various reports, 1996

OTHER INFORMATION

The Handbook of Emerging Markets: A Country-by-Country Guide to the World's Fastest Growing Economies, Robert Lloyd George, Probus Publishing, 1994

The Big Emerging Markets, published by United States Department of Commerce, Washington, D.C., Bernan Press, Md., 1995

The Financial Times, daily newspaper

Reuters, daily on-line news reports

Notes

Chapter 1
Who Are the Big Emerging Markets
and Why Are They Important?

Many of the general sources which I have used come from the Department of Commerce. They include research that had been done for speeches and public presentations which I made concerning the big emerging markets, as well as various aspects of international trade policy. Among them are: "The Big Emerging Markets: Changing American Interests in the Global Economy," January 20, 1994; "International Commercial Policy for the Twenty-first Century: Deepening Our Ties with the Big Emerging Markets," June 15, 1994; "Big Emerging Markets: New Thinking for a New World Order," March 9, 1995. All three were presented as a series at the Foreign Policy Association in New York. Another presentation was "Competing to Win in the Global Marketplace: If You Don't Win, You Lose," January 9, 1995, Council on Foreign Relations, N.Y. I have also made use of my public presentations on specific countries: "Rethinking U.S.-Indian Relations," March 22, 1994, Washington, D.C.; "India and America: A Partnership for the Twenty-first Century," November 18, 1994, Bombay; "The United States and Brazil: Partners in Change," March 29, 1994, São Paulo; "Forging a Deeper Commercial Relationship with Argentina," September 13, 1994, Washington, D.C.; "Expanding Opportunities for Commercial Ties Between the United States and China," Washington, D.C., November 3, 1994, "The Future of Commercial Engagement: America and China in a Time of Change," April 10, 1995, Beijing; and "Turkey: A Pivotal Big Emerging Market," August 31, 1995,

Istanbul. I have also relied heavily on these specific public reports: *The Big Emerging Markets: 1996 Outlook and Sourcebook* (Bernan Press, Md.); *National Export Strategy*, Report to Congress, October 1994 by the administration's Trade Promotion Coordinating Committee (known as the T.P.P.C. Reports); *National Export Strategy* Report 1995; *National Export Strategy* Report 1996; *U.S. Global Trade Outlook 1995–2000*, U.S. Department of Commerce, 1995; *1996 National Estimate Report on Foreign Trade Barriers*, U.S. Trade Representative (Washington, D.C., Government Printing Office, 1996). In addition I have drawn on several reports from international organizations, including annual reports of the International Monetary Fund and the World Trade Organization. For anyone interested in following the big emerging markets carefully, the two best sources are the daily *Financial Times* and the weekly *Economist*, two excellent and easily readable British publications which I used extensively for background information.

Books I read that were particularly valuable in shaping my thinking were: Karl Polanyi, *The Great Transformation: The Political and Economic Origins of Our Time*, Beacon Press, New York, 1957; Thomas S. Kuhn, *The Structure of Scientific Revolutions* (University of Chicago Press, 1970).

Chapter 2
The Rewards of Economic Engagement

A Cold Peace: America, Japan, Germany, and the Struggle for Supremacy was published in 1992 by Times Books (1993 in paper). For information on the importance of exports, see "Why Exports Are Worth Promoting," by J. David Richardson, a paper presented to a Council on Foreign Relations study group, November 19, 1996. Economic prospects for East Asia are discussed in many publications and articles, including *The Rise of China: How Economic Reform Is Creating a New Superpower*, by William H. Overholt, Norton, New York, 1993, and "The Pacific Century," by Andrew Tanzer, *Forbes*, July 15, 1996, pp. 109–113. For information regarding the potential growth of the BEMs, see "Linkages: O.E.C.D. and Major Developing Countries" by O.E.C.D., Paris, April 20, 1995. U.S. export prospects to the BEMs are discussed in several of the *National Export Strategy* reports to Congress and the *U.S. and Global Trade Outlook* report. See, for example, the T.P.C.C. report, October 1994, pp. 59–60. Latin American infrastructure requirements were reported in "Infrastructure in Latin America," by Stephen Fidler, *Financial Times*, September 13, 1996, Survey, p. 1. "Big emerging sectors" are discussed in the 1994 T.P.C.C. Report on National Export Strategy 1994 (op. cit.), pp. 62–65. For discussion of U.S. holdings of foreign stocks, see "Foreign Stocks Snapped Up by Americans," Michael R. Sesit, *Wall Street Journal*, February 6, 1996, p. 15. For estimates of emerging market equities held by Americans, see, for example, "U.S. Equity Flows to Emerging Markets," by Ryan Krueger, Nomura Securities, February 1996. Pension fund numbers come from "Global Investing," by John Warner, *Business Week*, September 9, 1996, p. 80, and "The Coming Global Pension Crisis," by Marshall N. Carter and William G. Shipman, *Foreign Affairs*, November/December 1996. The trip by state treasurers to East Asia was reported in "States Tap Asia for Better Returns on Pension Money," by Pui-Wing Tam, *Wall Street Journal*, September 3, 1996. Information regarding demand for automobiles in emerging markets can be found in "Car Makers Look Beyond Established Markets," by Haig Simonian, *Financial Times*, July 12, 1996, p. 3; "South American Trade Pact Is Under Fire," by Michael M. Phillips, *Wall Street Journal*, October 23, 1996, p. A2; "A Traffic Jam of Auto Makers," by Jim Flynn and Katherine Anne Miller, August 5, 1996, p. 47. For information on Coca-Cola's plans, see "Coke Pours Into Asia," by Mark L. Clifford et al., *Business Week*, October 28, 1996, p. 72; for information on defense contractors, see "U.S. Defense Contractors Lick Chops for Latin Market," by Jonathan Friedland, *Wall Street Journal*, November 15, 1996, p. A10; for Morgan Stanley's plans, see "Global Gamble," by Leah Natan Spiro et al., *Business Week*, February 12, 1996; for Citibank see "The Ante Raises in East Asia," by Susan Hansel, *New York Times*, July 14, 1996, Section 3, p. 1.

Chapter 3
The Risks of Economic Engagement

For views concerning the dramatic new world that is arising, including the number of new producers and consumers coming on stream in the world economy, see "Will the 1990s Be the Second Great Age of Global Capitalism?" by David Hale, Kemper Financial Services, June

1992; "Capitalism Isn't Broken," by Michael C. Jensen and Perry Fagan, *Wall Street Journal*, March 3, 1996, p. A10; and especially "War of the Worlds," a survey by Pam Woodall, *The Economist*, October 1, 1994. An excellent article on the rise of emerging markets and the structural changes that will follow is "Power and Policy: The New Economic World Order," by Klaus Schwab and Claude Smadja, *Harvard Business Review*, November/December 1994. Data on wages came from Morgan Stanley research as reported in "Sliding Scales," *The Economist*, November 2, 1996, p. 77. Concerning potential productivity in emerging markets, I conducted a phone interview with Professor Michael Jansen at the Harvard Business School, who had made an extensive trip to Asia for research on this subject and who himself conducted interviews with managers in the region. The quote from Michael Porter comes from *Competitiveness Index 1996: A Ten-Year Strategic Assessment*, by the Council on Competitiveness, Washington, D.C., October 1996, p. 1. Information on Singapore's drive to attract new firms in high-value-added industries is discussed in "This Island Is Crazy for Chips," by Mark L. Clifford, *Business Week*, September 16, 1996, p. 58. Workers petitioning for trade adjustment because of NAFTA comes from "NAFTA Transitional Adjustment Assistance," Historical Summary, 1996 (handout). The Samsung story in Mexico is described in "Economics Lessons in a Border Town," by Anthony DePalma, *New York Times*, May 23, 1996, p. D5. For information on mergers and acquisitions in Brazil, see "The Buying and Selling of Brazil Inc.," *The Economist*, November 9, 1996, p. 83. The survey of American executives on the Coucil on Competitiveness is described in *Competitiveness Index 1996: A Ten-Year Strategic Assessment*, Council on Competitiveness, Washington, D.C., October 1996. Studies concerning trade and foreign investment are discussed in the 1996 Annual Report of the World Trade Organization, Geneva, December 1996. The McDonnell Douglas story in China was reported in "Aircraft Deal with Chinese Is Questioned," by Jeff Gerth and David Sanger, *New York Times*, Wednesday, October 30, 1996, p. 1. An excellent source on intellectual property rights in China is *To Steal a Book Is an Elegant Offense: Intellectual Property Law in Chinese Civilization*, by William P. Alfond (Stanford University Press, 1995). For more general information on losses due to I.P.R. violations, see "Cops Versus Robers in Cyberspace," by Philip E. Ross, *Forbes*, September 9, 1996, p. 134.

On corruption in Mexico, see "Crime Wave Leaves Mexicans Wary of Federal Police," by Sam Dillon, *New York Times*, September 3, 1996, p. A4. Information of losses to U.S. firms due to corruption can be found in the T.P.C.C. Report on National Export Strategy of October 1996. Regarding returns on emerging markets investments, I used research from J. P. Morgan and the International Finance Corporation. See also: "Hot Emerging Bond Funds Leave Some Investors Cold," by Charles Gesparco, *Wall Street Journal*, November 6, 1996, p. C1.

Chapter 4
Beyond Economics: Political Power and Political Instability

The *Foreign Affairs* article cited is "The Myth of Post–Cold War Chaos," by G. John Ikenberry, May/June, 1996. For nationalism in emerging markets, see "The West: Unique, Not Universal," by Samuel P. Huntington, *Foreign Affairs*, November/December 1996, p. 37. The quote from an Indian newspaper is from *The Hindu*, as reported in "India Unites Over Nuclear Arms Stance," by Shiraz Sidhva, *Financial Times*, August 22, 1996, p. 5. Sources for reserves are the International Monetary Fund's "International Finance Statistics," and *The Economist*. On the scramble for energy, see *Pacific Defense: Arms, Energy, and America's Future in Asia*, by Kent Calder, William Morrow, New York, 1996). A thoughtful observer of the relationship between democracy and economic development, or democracy and the behavior of nations is Samuel P. Huntington. I was greatly influenced many years ago by Huntington's book, *Political Order in Changing Societies* (Yale University Press, 1968), and have drawn on several of his articles for this book, including "Democracy for the Long Haul," in the *Journal of Democracy,* April, 1996. The Donald Kagan quote is found in "Democracy and the National Interest," by Strobe Talbott, *Foreign Affairs*, November/December 1996, p. 2. Information on income inequality in Mexico was reported in "Income Gulf in Mexico Grows and So Do Protests," by Anthony DePalma, *New York Times*, July 21, 1996, p. 3. Indonesia quote comes from "A Time of Living Dangerously," by Manuela Saragosa, *Financial Times*, September 3, 1996, p. 13. On South Africa, see "A Nation Under Siege," by Kathy Chenault, *Business Week*, September 30,

1996, p. 54, and "South African Survey," by Roger Matthews, *Financial Times*, October 3, 1996. Other sources that I drew on in this chapter include Andres Oppenheimer, *Bordering on Chaos: Guerrillas, Stockbrokers, Politicians, and Mexico's Road to Prosperity*, (Little, Brown, Boston, 1996), as well as various country analyses done by the *Financial Times* and *The Economist*.

Chapter 5
Clashes with American Values

Information on labor standards and human rights comes from *Country Reports on Human Rights Practices for 1993*, submitted to the U.S. Congress by the Department of State, April 1996. See also "Amnesty Launches Turkish Human Rights Campaign," Reuter, October 1, 1996; "Brazil: Fighting Violence with Violence," Human Rights Watch, Americas, January 1996; "The Limits of Openness: Human Rights in Indonesia and East Timor," Human Rights Watch/Asia, September 1994. Reference to the International Labor Organization Report on Child Labor is from "Estimate of Child-Labor Levels Triples," by G. Pascal Zachary, *Wall Street Journal*, November 12, 1996, p. A2. The Mahathir quote comes from "The West: Unique, Not Universal," by Samuel P. Huntington, *Foreign Affairs*, November/December 1996, p. 41.

Sources for environmental issues are as follows: "The Future of Populous Economies," by Robert Livernash, *Environment*, July 1995, p. 6; *Environmental Issues in Chemical Perspective*, by Thomas Spiro and William Stigliani (Kendall/Hunt Publishing, Dubuque, Iowa, 1990), pp. 107, 109; "Loss of Species Is Worse Than Thought in the Amazon," by William K. Stevens, *New York Times*, June 29, 1993, p. 4; "Threats to Biodiversity," by Edward O. Wilson, in *Managing the Planet* (W. H. Freeman Co., New York, 1990), pp. 49–53; "Where Are the New Diseases Born?" by Anne Gibbons, *Science*, August 6, 1993, pp. 680–81; "Hugh Material and Human Cost of Environmental Damage in Poland," Polish News Bulletin, March 10, 1996, p. 50; "The West May Need Help— Plant Closures Have Reduced Pollution But. . . " by Anthony Robinson, *Financial Times*, November 20, 1990. I am also indebted to Michael Oppenheimer of Multinational Strategies, who shared with me extensive research material he had gathered and summarized on populational and environmental trends, and their relationship to geopolitics.

Chapter 6
America Unprepared

The quotes from presidents come from *The Annals of America*, published by the Encyclopedia Britannica, 1976, Vol. 3, pp. 614, 615; Vol. 4, p. 144; *Ideals and Self-Interest in America's Foreign Relations*, by Robert Osgood, University of Chicago Press, 1958, p. 296; *Ned Gordon Levin, Jr., Woodrow Wilson and World Politics*, Oxford University, 1968 p. 17.

The Chicago survey's formal title is "American Public Opinion and U.S. Foreign Policy 1995," Chicago Council on Foreign Relations, edited by John E. Rielly. Quotes by Secretaries Christopher and Rubin are from official press releases.

Information on savings and investment comes from the bipartisan Competitiveness Policy Council, Washington, D.C. On income inequalities and wage stagnation, see "Toward an Apartheid Economy," by Richard B. Freeman, *Harvard Business Review*, September/October 1996, p. 115; also see "Running in Place: Recent Trends in U.S. Living Standards," Competitiveness Policy Council. On health coverage, see *America Needs a Raise*, by John J. Sweeney (Houghton Mifflin, New York, 1996), p. 36, and "Firms Cut Health Costs," by David Wessell, *Wall Street Journal*, November 11, 1996, p. 1. On displaced workers suffering wage declines, see "The Gates of Creative Destruction: Embracing Change in the U.S. Economy," speech by Dr. Joseph E. Stiglitz, Chairman, White House Council of Economic Advisors, at Boston University, June 3, 1996. Contingent workforce numbers are from *America Needs a Raise*, p. 36. For discussion of public infrastructure needs, see "Investing in Our Future: Report of the Public Infrastructure Subcouncil to the Competitiveness Policy Council," March 1993. Moynihan quote is found in "When Principle Is at Stake," article by Daniel Patrick Moynihan on the op-ed page of the *Washington Post*, August 4, 1996. The Felix Rohatyn quote is from "Recipe for Growth," *Wall Street Journal*, April 11, 1996, p. A18.

Chapter 7
Restructuring Our Policies at Home

Employment numbers come from, "Letting the Good Times Roll: The Case Against a Rate Rise," by Peter Passell, *New York Times*, September 12, 1996, p. 1. For a discussion about the severity of the entitlements problem, see *Will America Grow Up Before It Grows Old? How the Coming Social Security Crisis Threatens You, Your Family, and Your Country*, by Peter G. Peterson (Random House, New York, 1996). Information on deregulation can be found in "Tomorrow's Economic Adjustment," *The Economist*, July 27, 1996, p. 19; a report by the General Accounting Office of Congress on "Airline Deregulation," April 19, 1996; "Regulation and Its Impact on Competitiveness," Competitiveness Policy Council, September 1995; and "Electricity: The Power Shift Ahead," by Peter Coy and Gary McWilliams, *Business Week*, December 2, 1996, p. 78. On infrastructure, see the GAO report, "Condition of America's Schools," September 19, 1994, and "National Plan of Integrated Airport Systems: Report to Congress," submitted by the U.S. Department of Transportation, April 1995, and "Gas Tax Could Help Our Cities," by Felix Rohatyn, *New York Times*, September 11, 1996, p. A19. On Federal Reserve policy, see "The Fed Should Keep Its Head," by Robert Eisner, *New York Times*, September 19, 1996, p. A27, and Felix Rohatyn, "Clinton's Growth Agenda," *Wall Street Journal*, September 16, 1996, p. A18. Productivity and workers' compensation figures come from "The Hollow Ring of the Productivity Revival," by Stephen S. Roach, *Harvard Business Review*, November/December 1996, p. 86. Educational statistics come from the *1995 Digest of Education Statistics*, plus *Report of the Institute of International Education*, December 2, 1996, Washington, D.C.

Chapter 8
A Vigorous Commercial Diplomacy

Reference to Coca-Cola comes from "Coke Pours Into Asia," by Mark L. Clifford et al., *Business Week*, October 28, 1996, p. 72. The Raymond Smith quote is from, "Business as War Game: A Report from the Battlefront," by Raymond W. Smith, *Fortune*, September 30, 1996, p. 190. An excellent overview of the issues involved in China's entry into the WTO is

"China and the WTO," by Nicholas R. Lardy, The Brookings Institution, November 1996. Information on foreign reporting, including the Zuckerman quote, comes from "Foreign Coverage Less Prominent in News Magazines," by Robin Pogrebin, *New York Times*, September 23, 1996, p. D2. For extensive information on trade promotion, see the four public reports to Congress, 1993, 1994, 1995, 1996, entitled, "National Export Strategy," by the administration's trade promotion coordinating committee.

Chapter 9
America's Choice

The Bismarck quote is found in William Safire, *Lend Me Your Ears: Great Speeches in History* (W. W. Norton, New York, 1992), p. 888.

Index